ZOOM IN ...
Globalization

Herausgegeben von:
Iris Faßbender und Colette Granvillano

Erarbeitet von:
Monika M. Jäger

Schöningh

Muttersprachliche Betreuung: Ronnie Halligan

© 2016 Bildungshaus Schulbuchverlage
Westermann Schroedel Diesterweg Schöningh Winklers GmbH
Braunschweig, Paderborn, Darmstadt

www.schoeningh-schulbuch.de
Schöningh Verlag, Jühenplatz 1–3, 33098 Paderborn

Druck 5 4 3 2 1 / Jahr 2020 19 18 17 16
Alle Drucke der Serie A sind im Unterricht parallel verwendbar.
Die letzte Zahl bezeichnet das Jahr dieses Druckes.

Umschlaggestaltung: Reinhild Kassing, Kassel
Umschlagabbildung: © Justin Foulkes/4Corners/Schapowalow
Druck und Bindung: westermann druck GmbH, Braunschweig

ISBN 978-3-14-040658-1

Zur Arbeit mit dem Buch

Anforderungsbereiche

Alle Aufgaben dieses Bandes sind farbig gekennzeichnet und sind somit den drei Anforderungsbereichen eindeutig zuzuordnen. Eine detaillierte Aufstellung aller Operatoren finden Sie im Anhang.

➡ AFB I: Comprehension

➡ AFB II: Analysis

➡ AFB III: Evaluation/Re-creation of text

➡ Aufgaben, die einen Text inhaltlich/sprachlich vorbereiten beziehungsweise weiterführend vertiefen, sind grau unterlegt.

Symbole

Auf verschiedenen Seiten dieses Bandes finden Sie Symbole, die auf sprachlich-methodische Fertigkeiten, Musterlösungen und weiterführende Aktivitäten hinweisen.

 Speaking – Mithilfe dieser Aufgabe wird der mündliche Ausdruck geübt.

 Listening – Zu diesem Material gibt es im Lehrerband eine Audio-Datei (auf CD), mit der das Hörverstehen geschult wird.

 Mediation – Dieses Material wird in eigenen Worten auf Englisch bzw. auf Deutsch wiedergegeben und dient der Sprachmittlung.

 Model solution – Zu dieser Aufgabe liegt eine Musterlösung vor.

 Activity – Bei dieser Aufgabe werden die Schülerinnen und Schüler in vielfältiger Weise selbst aktiv.

Webcodes

Webcodes verweisen auf Zusatzmaterial im Internet und erleichtern Ihnen das Auffinden von Links und Dateien, die speziell für den vorliegenden Band ausgewählt oder erstellt wurden.

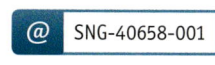 @ SNG-40658-001

Zur Nutzung gehen Sie bitte auf folgende Seite: http://www.schoeningh-schulbuch.de/webcodes

Geben Sie dort den Code ein, um zu dem jeweiligen Material zu gelangen.

Contents

Getting started

Students from all over the world attending an international business school in Bad Honnef, Germany

Some milestones of globalization:

1980s	1987	1989	1991	1992	1996	2001
The first cases of **AIDS** are identified in the U.S. and the discovery of **HIV** is made soon after.	The **Stock Market Crash** on Wall Street spreads overnight. The appearance of an **ozone hole** over Antarctica raises global ecological awareness.	The **fall of the Berlin Wall** ultimately leads to the collapse of the Soviet Union and the end of the Cold War.	The **World Wide Web** is introduced as a global information service operating over the Internet.	**The EU** is established, introducing intergovernmental cooperation to the economic and political communities.	The first **GM crop** is harvested. **Dolly the Sheep** is born, which sparks ethical debates worldwide.	**9/11**, a series of terrorist attacks by the Islamic group al-Qaeda on the U.S., initiates the **Global War on Terrorism**.

Civil   Kind   Outward looking   Honest
"I take responsibility"   "What can I do to help?"
                    "I'm listening"
"I can see
different   **Open Minded**   Gets involved
points of view"
     Aware   Social   Compassionate
          "I'm Curious"   Part of the community
Friendly   **Political**
     Understanding   Proactive/tenacious
Awareness of   "I want to stay
place in the world   informed"
                         Openness
"I'm working   "The worlds a
together in   small place"
partnership"
                    Knowledge hungry
     Curious   -willing to learn
Empathy   **Educated**
     Accepting   Multi Lingual
"I know & value   Socially Aware
my own culture"   Optimistic
"I'm respective of others"   "I want to find out"
Aware of news and issues   Curious about other cultures
in other countries   and interested to learn
          Respectful   Responsible

ZOOM IN: Vocabulary

civil polite, courteous
compassionate feeling
sympathy for people who are
suffering
tenacious determined to do
something even when it
becomes difficult

➡ Describe the photograph and the drawing and explain what links the two
visuals. Then ask yourself whether you meet any of the criteria identifying
you as a global citizen.

2005	2008/2009	2010	2011	2010–2015	2013–2015	2015
The **Kyoto Protocol**, acknowledging the existence and causes of global warming, enters into force.	The **financial crisis** illustrates the failure of institutions to manage systemic risk and keep pace with globalization.	The **Arab Spring** starts with protests via social media against state repression and Internet censorship.	The Fukushima nuclear disaster triggers a **nuclear power retrenchment**. Germany even phases out.	**Boko Haram, ISIS** and **al-Qaeda** are terrorising Nigeria, Iraq and Syria, which results in increased waves of migration.	The most severe **Ebola outbreak** ever begins in Guinea and spreads abroad where it is still ongoing.	The **Charlie Hebdo** massacre in Paris manifests the blatant clash of globalization and ideologies.

Dani Rodrik

M1 A Bedtime Story for Grown-ups

Dani Rodrik

Dani Rodrik (born in Istanbul, Turkey, in 1957) is a professor at Harvard University who harshly criticises today's "maximum globalization". To his mind, globalization will only work for everyone if all countries comply with the same rules. If these rules are embedded within social, legal and political institutions that provide them with legitimacy, globalization will be "smart", as Rodrik calls it, and allow the benefits of capitalism to be broadly shared.

1. Before starting to read, look at the title of the story and the heading of this chapter. Speculate on what the story could be about.

2. After reading the so-called 'bedtime story', use the fishbone diagram (cf. skills pages) for listing the difficulties the villagers encounter (on one side of the diagram) and the responses to these difficulties (on the opposite side).

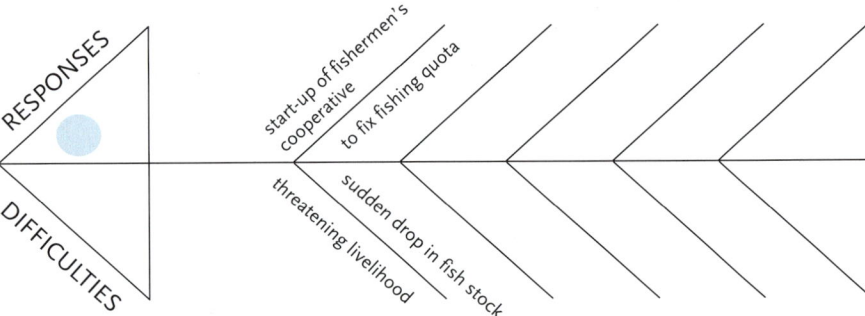

3. Based on your fishbone diagram, **summarise** what changes the little fishing village went through in order to make everyone live happily ever after.

4. **Examine** the means Rodrik uses to convince the reader of his concept of 'smart globalization'. Focus on the role of the shaman, the council of elders and the villagers as well as on the type and purpose of the text.

5. **Comment** on the story's closing formula "And everyone lived happily ever after." In your comment, you should include your opinion on whether "the vicious cycle" (l. 12) that the villagers were caught in will be interrupted in the long run.

Once upon a time there was a little fishing village at the edge of a lake. The villagers were poor, living off the fish they caught and the clothing they sewed. They had no

5 contact with the other inland villages, which were miles away and reached only after days of travel through a dense forest. Life for the villagers took a turn for the worse when the stock of fish in the lake

10 plummeted*. Villagers responded by working harder, but they were caught in a vicious cycle*. The scarcer the fish got, the longer the hours that each fisherman spent on the lake, which in turn depleted* the fish stock at an even faster rate.

15 The villagers went to the village shaman* and asked for help. He shrugged and said, "What is our council of elders for? They sit around all day and do nothing but gossip. They should solve this problem." "How?" the villagers asked. "Simple," he said. "The council should set up a fishermen's cooperative that decides how much fish each man can catch in a month. The fish stock will be renewed and we will not run into this problem in the future."

20 The council of elders did as the shaman suggested. The villagers weren't happy that the elders told them how to run their business, but they understood the need for the restraint*. In no time, the lake was overflowing with fish.

The villagers returned to the shaman. They bowed in front of him and thanked him for his wisdom. Just as they were leaving, the shaman said: "Since you seem to be interested

25 in my help, would you like me to give you another idea?" "Of course," the villagers cried in unison*.

"Well," the shaman said. "Isn't it crazy that you all have to spend so much of your time sewing your own clothes when you could buy much better and cheaper ones from the villages on the other side of the forest? They aren't easy to get to, but you would only have

30 to make the trip once or twice a year."

"Oh, but what can we sell in return?" asked the villagers. "I hear the people inland love dried fish," said the shaman.

to plummet to drop suddenly in amount
vicious ['vɪʃəs] **cycle** a chain of events in which the response to one difficulty creates a new problem that makes the original difficulty even more severe
to deplete to reduce in quantity
shaman ['ʃæmən] someone who acts as a medium between the visible world and an invisible spirit world and who practises magic for purposes of healing, divination, and control over natural events
restraint a way of limiting or controlling something
in unison all at the same time, in agreement

garment a piece of clothing
livelihood a way of earning money in order to live
squeeze *here:* financial pressure caused by narrowing margins

discord lack of agreement between people

in droves in large numbers

onerous *here:* burdensome, excessive

to evade to avoid

boisterous very lively

unsustainable untenable, unworkable, not able to be supported in the future
boulder a very large stone

tollbooth a small building where you pay a toll to use a road or bridge

And that is what the villagers did. They dried some of their fish and started to trade with the villages on the other side of the forest. The fishermen got rich on the high prices they received while the price of garments* in the village dropped sharply. 35

Not all villagers were happy. Those who did not own a boat and whose livelihood* depended on the garments they sewed were caught in a squeeze*. They had to compete with the cheaper and higher-quality garments brought in from the other villages and had a harder time getting their hands on cheap fish. They asked the shaman what they should do.

"Well, this is another problem for the council of elders to solve," said the shaman. "You 40 know how every family has to make a contribution during our monthly feast?" "Yes," they replied.

"Well, since the fishermen are now so much richer, they should make a bigger contribution and you should make less."

The council of elders thought this was fair and they asked the fishermen to increase their 45 monthly contribution. The fishermen weren't thrilled, but it seemed like a sensible thing to do to avoid discord* in the village. Soon the rest of the village was happy, too.

The shaman meanwhile had another idea. He said: "Imagine how much richer our village could be if our traders did not have to spend days travelling through the dense forest. Imagine how much more trade we could have if there was a regular road through the for- 50 est." "But how?" asked the villagers. "Simple," said the shaman. "The council of elders should organize work brigades to cut through the forest and lay down a road."

Before long, the village was connected to the other villages by a paved road that cut down on travel time and cost. Trade expanded and the fishermen got even richer, but they didn't neglect to share their riches with the other villagers at feast time. 55

As time passed, however, things turned sour. The road gave villagers from beyond the forest easy access to the lake and allowed them to take up fishing, which they did in droves*. Since neither the council nor the fishermen's cooperative could enforce the fishing restrictions on outsiders, the fish stock began to deplete rapidly again.

The new competition also cut into the earnings of the local fishermen. They began to 60 complain about the feast tax being too onerous*. "How can we compete effectively with the outsiders who are not subject to similar requirements?" they asked in desperation. Some local fishermen even made a habit of absenting themselves from the village on feast days – the road had made it easy to come and go – and evaded* their obligations altogether. This made the rest of the villagers furious. 65

It was time for another trip to the shaman. The village held a long and boisterous* meeting at which each side argued its case passionately. All agreed that the situation was unsustainable*, but the proposed solutions varied. The fishermen wanted a change in the rules that would reduce their contributions to the monthly feasts. Others wanted an end to the fish trade with outsiders. Some even asked to blockade the road with boulders* so 70 that no one could enter or leave the village.

The shaman listened to these arguments. "You have to be reasonable and compromise," he said after some thought. "Here is what I suggest. The council of elders should place a tollbooth* at the entrance to the access road, and everyone who comes in and out should pay a fee." "But this will make it more costly for us to trade," the fishermen objected. "Yes, 75 indeed," the shaman replied. "But it will also reduce overfishing and make up for the loss in contributions at the feasts. And it won't cut off trade altogether," he added, pointing with his head to the villagers who wanted to block the road.

The villagers agreed that this was a reasonable solution. They walked out of the meeting satisfied. Harmony was restored to the village. 80

And everyone lived happily ever after.

Dani Rodrik, *The Globalization Paradox: Democracy and the Future of the World Economy*, W. W. Norton, New York 2012, Afterword

ZOOM IN: People

Thomas L. Friedman, (born in Minneapolis, U.S., in 1953) is an internationally renowned author, reporter and columnist, the recipient of three Pulitzer Prizes and the author of several bestselling books.

Joseph E. Stiglitz (born in Gary, U.S., in 1943) is an economist and a professor at Columbia University. In 2001, he received the Nobel Memorial Prize in Economic Sciences.

M2 What Exactly Is Globalization?

Thomas L. Friedman/Joseph E. Stiglitz

1. ⟩⟩ Read the two definitions of globalization very thoroughly, then identify and define any unfamiliar term. Make sure you fully understand the two quotations.

2. ⟩⟩ Have a close look at the flow chart (cf. skills pages) that represents Friedman's ideas visually. Now it is your turn to map Stiglitz's ideas in a similar manner.

3. ⟩⟩ **State** briefly to what extent the definitions coincide.

4. ⟩⟩ **Compare** Friedman and Stiglitz's choice of words and syntax and **point out** the main differences and their effect.

"I define globalization as the inexorable integration of markets, transportation systems, and
5 communication systems [...] in a way that is enabling corporations, countries, and individuals to reach around the
10 world farther, faster, deeper, and cheaper than ever before, and in a way that is enabling the world to reach into corporations, countries, and
15 individuals farther, faster, deeper, and cheaper than ever before."

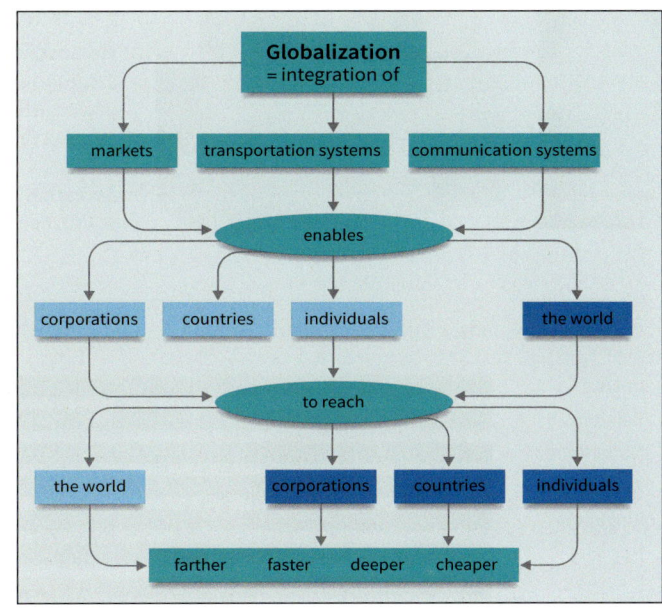

Thomas L. Friedman, *Longitudes and Attitudes: Exploring the World after September 11*, Farrar, Straus & Giroux, New York 2002, p. 3

"Fundamentally, it is the closer integration of the countries and peoples of the world which has been brought about by the enormous reduction of costs of transportation and communication and the breaking down of artificial barriers to the flows of goods, services, capital, knowledge, and (to a lesser extent) people across borders."

Joseph E. Stiglitz, *Globalization and Its Discontent*, Penguin, London 2003, p. 9

index (*sg.*), **indices** (*pl.*) ['ɪndəsiz] number/s derived from a series of observations and used as indicator/s or measure **proximity** closeness

5. Watch a short clip on *YouTube* (see Webcode) that explains and illustrates what exactly globalization is. If necessary, skim the transcript to fill in any gaps in understanding. Then prepare to explain the concept of globalization to your classmates.

6. Have a look at the statistics showing the most globalized countries (out of 207). The index* measures the three main dimensions of globalization: economic, social and political. In addition to three indices* measuring these dimensions, there is an overall index of globalization and sub-indices for actual economic flows and restrictions as well as data on information flows, personal contact and cultural proximity*. For the purpose of these statistics, globalization is defined as "the process of creating networks of connections among actors at multi-continental distances, mediated through a variety of flows including people, information and ideas, capital and goods". Does this ranking list of globalized countries measure up to your expectations? **Justify** your answer.

Multinational companies such as *Starbucks*, *amazon* and *Google* have come under fire for paying little or no corporation income tax because they transfer offshore profits to sister companies in tax-friendly countries (*Starbucks* to the Netherlands, *amazon* to Luxembourg, *Google* to Ireland).

Top countries in the Globalization Index 2014 (top five and selection)

Country	Index
Ireland	92.17
Belgium	91.61
Netherlands	91.33
Austria	90.48
Singapore	88.63
Hungary	85.91
Canada	85.63
United Kingdom	83.72
Germany	79.47
New Zealand	78.82
Malta	75.95
United States	74.94

Data: KOF Swiss Economic Institute/ETH Zürich

ZOOM IN: People

Albert Arnold "Al" Gore, Jr (born in Washington, D.C., in 1948) is a politician, advocate and philanthropist, who served as the 45th Vice President of the United States (1993–2001) under President Bill Clinton. He has founded a number of non-profit organisations, including the Alliance for Climate Protection, and has received a Nobel Peace Prize for his work in climate change activism.

M3 Earth Inc.

Al Gore

1. Before reading, brainstorm in class: What do you already know about the 'outsourcing' of jobs? Do you have any idea why the term has a strongly negative connotation among both jobholders and job seekers?

ZOOM IN: Terminology

Denotation refers to the literal meaning of a word, i.e. the 'dictionary definition'. **Connotation**, however, refers to the associations or emotional suggestions that are connected to a certain word.

2. **Outline** how and why, according to Al Gore, the global economy is changing profoundly at a very fast rate.

3. **Explain** the meaning of the term "Earth Inc." in this context.

4. **Analyse** Al Gore's attitude towards the transformation of the global economy. Focus on his line of argument and use of stylistic devices.

5. "Psychologically, emotionally, and in the ways we frame our identity, most of us still think and act as if we are still living in the world we knew when we were young. In fact, however, where the economic realities of life are concerned, that world is receding from view." **Discuss**.

The global economy is being transformed by changes far greater in speed and scale than any in human history. We are living with, and in, Earth Inc.*: national policies, regional strategies, and long accepted economic theories are now irrelevant to the new realities of our new hyper-connected, tightly integrated, highly interactive, and technologically revo-
5 lutionized economy.
Many of the most successful large enterprises in the world now produce goods in "virtual global factories," with intricate* spiderwebs of supply chains connecting to hundreds of other enterprises in dozens of countries. More and more markets for goods – and increasingly services that do not require face-to-face interaction – are now global in nature. High-
10 er and higher percentages of wage earners must now compete not only with wage earners in every other country, but also with intelligent machines interconnected with other machines and computer networks.

Inc. = Incorporated the founding of a corporation, i.e. a business firm with a corporate structure

intricate difficult to analyse

metastasis [mɪˈtæstəsɪs]
here: a change of state or form
to emerge to rise from an inferior position or condition

efficacy [ˈɛfɪkəsɪ]
efficiency, productiveness, performance

entity something that has an independent and separate existence
momentum the force that something has when it is moving

to frame to shape

to recede to withdraw

to come to grips with to deal with straightforwardly, to cope with

The digitization of work and the dramatic and relatively sudden metastasis* of what used to be called automation are driving two massive changes simultaneously:
1. the outsourcing of jobs from industrial economies to developing and emerging* econo- 15
mies with large populations and lower wages; and
2. the robosourcing of jobs from human beings to mechanized processes, computer programs, robots of all sizes and shapes, and still rudimentary versions of artificial intelligence that are improving in their efficacy*, utility, and power with each passing year.
The transformation of the global economy is best understood as an emergent phenome- 20
non – that is, one in which the whole is not only greater than the sum of its parts, but very different from the sum of its parts in important and powerful ways. It represents something new – not just a more interconnected collection of the same national and regional economies that used to interact with one another, but a completely new entity* with different internal dynamics, patterns, momentum*, and raw power than what we have been 25
familiar with in the past. There are limits to cross-border flows of people, of course, and trade flows are stronger among countries that are close to one another, but the entire global economy has been knit together much more tightly than ever before.
Just as the thirteen American colonies in North America emerged as a unified whole in the last quarter of the eighteenth century – and just as the ancient walled city-states of 30
Italy eventually became a unified nation in the second half of the nineteenth century – the world as a whole has now emerged as a single economic entity that is moving quickly toward full integration. At least that is the reality in the world of commerce and industry, in the world of science, and in the rapid spreading of most new technologies to centers of commerce throughout the world. 35
In the world of politics and governmental policy, nation-states remain the dominant players. Psychologically, emotionally, and in the ways we frame* our identity, most of us still think and act as if we are still living in the world we knew when we were young. In fact, however, where the economic realities of life are concerned, that world is receding* from view. 40
This powerful driver of global change – sometimes loosely and inadequately referred to as "globalization" – marks not only the end of one era in history and the beginning of another, it marks the emergence of a completely new reality with which we as human beings must come to grips*.

Al Gore, *The Future: Six Drivers of Global Change*, Random House, New York 2013, pp. 4/5

M4   A Hologram for the King

Dave Eggers

In the opening chapter of Eggers's novel *A Hologram for the King*, we are taken around the world with Alan Clay, the protagonist, who is fighting to hold himself and his splintering family together in the face of the global economy's adversities.

1. **Describe** the situation of the protagonist and the changes he has had to cope with.

2. **Analyse** the way the protagonist is presented to the reader. Focus on the narrative perspective, content and language.

3. *A Hologram for the King* is set in a newly globalized world in which jobs are outsourced abroad. With reference to this novel excerpt and to that from Al Gore's recent book (cf. M 3), **assess** how globalization affects – for good or ill – the lives of individuals throughout the world.

4. ⟩ Put yourself in the shoes of Alan Clay sitting at Nairobi Airport, talking to the woman from upstate New York about the consequences of the decisions he has made in his life. Write their dialogue.

Alan Clay woke up in Jeddah, Saudi Arabia. It was May 30, 2010. He had spent two days on planes to get there.

In Nairobi he had met a woman. They sat next to each other while they waited for their flights. She was tall, curvy, with tiny gold earrings. She had ruddy* skin and a lilting*
5   voice. Alan liked her more than many of the people in his life, people he saw every day. She said she lived in upstate New York. Not that far away from his home in suburban Boston.

If he had courage he would have found a way to spend more time with her. But instead he got on his flight and he flew to Riyadh and then to Jeddah. A man picked him up at the
10   airport and drove him to the Hilton.

With a click, Alan entered his room at the Hilton at 1:12 a.m. He quickly prepared to go to bed. He needed to sleep. He had to travel an hour north at seven for an eight o'clock arrival at the King Abdullah Economic City. There he and his team would set up a holographic* teleconference system and would wait to present it to King Abdullah himself. If
15   Abdullah was impressed, he would award the IT contract for the entire city to Reliant*, and Alan's commission, in the mid-six figures, would fix everything that ailed* him.

So he needed to feel rested. To feel prepared. But instead he had spent four hours in bed not sleeping.

He thought of his daughter Kit, who was in college, a very good and expensive college. He
20   did not have the money to pay her tuition for the fall. He could not pay her tuition because he had made a series of foolish decisions in his life. He had not planned well. He had not had courage when he needed it.

His decisions had been shortsighted.

The decisions of his peers had been shortsighted.
25   These decisions had been foolish and expedient*.

But he hadn't known at the time that his decisions were shortsighted, foolish or expedient. He and his peers did not know they were making decisions that would leave them, leave Alan, as he now was – virtually broke, nearly unemployed, the proprietor of a one-man consulting firm run out of his home office.
30   He was divorced from Kit's mother Ruby. They had now been apart longer than they had been together. Ruby was an unholy pain in the ass who now lived in California and contributed nothing financially to Kit's finances. College is *your* thing, she told him. Be a man about it, she said.

Now Kit would not be in college in the fall. Alan had put his house on the market but it
35   had not yet sold. Otherwise he was out of options. He owed money to many people, including $18k* to a pair of bicycle designers who had built him a prototype for a new bicycle he thought he could manufacture in the Boston area. For this he was called an idiot. He owed money to Jim Wong, who had loaned him $45k to pay for materials and the first and last on a warehouse lease. He owed another $65k or so to a half-dozen friends and
40   would-be partners.

So he was broke. And when he realized he could not pay Kit's tuition, it was too late to apply for any other aid. Too late to transfer.

Was it a tragedy that a healthy young woman like Kit would take a semester off of college? No, it was not a tragedy. The long, tortured history of the world would take no notice of a

Dave Eggers (born in Massachusetts, U.S., in 1970)

ruddy pink and healthy
lilting with a pleasant pattern of rising and falling sound

holographic (*adj.*),
hologram (*n.*) a special kind of picture that is produced by a laser and that looks three-dimensional
Reliant a power company that provides electricity to residents and businesses in the Dallas and Fort Worth Texas area
to ail (*old-fashioned*) to bother, to trouble, to make somebody feel ill or unhappy
expedient helping you to deal with a problem quickly and effectively although sometimes in a way that is not morally right

k (*informal*) an abbreviation for one thousand

missed semester of college for a smart and capable young woman like Kit. She would survive. It was no tragedy. Nothing like tragedy. [45]

They said it was a tragedy what had happened to Charlie Fallon. Charlie Fallon froze to death in the lake near Alan's house. The lake next to Alan's house.

Alan was thinking of Charlie Fallon while not sleeping in the room at the Jeddah Hilton. Alan had seen Charlie step into the lake that day. Alan was driving away, on his way to the [50] quarry*. It had not seemed normal that a man like Charlie Fallon would be stepping into the shimmering black lake in September, but neither was it extraordinary.

Charlie Fallon had been sending Alan pages from books. He had been doing this for two years. Charlie had discovered the Transcendentalists* late in life and felt a kinship* with them. He had seen that Brook Farm was not far from where he and Alan lived, and he [55] thought it meant something. He traced his Boston ancestry, hoping to find a connection, but found none. Still, he sent Alan pages, with passages highlighted.

The workings of a privileged mind, Alan thought. Don't send me more of that shit, he told Charlie. But Charlie grinned and sent more.

So when Alan saw Charlie stepping into the lake at noon on a Saturday he saw it as a [60] logical extension of the man's new passion for the land. He was only ankle-deep when Alan passed him that day.

Dave Eggers, *A Hologram for the King*, McSweeney's, San Francisco 2012, pp. 3–6

quarry ['kwɒrɪ] a place where large amounts of stone or sand are dug out of the ground
Transcendentalists a group of people who believe that knowledge can be obtained by studying thought rather than by practical experience
kinship a strong connection between people, relationship, affinity

---

M5 25 Years after Berlin, Do We Still Need Walls?

Peter Schurman

1. Before reading, ask your parents, grandparents, aunts and uncles, neighbours or acquaintances what they remember about (1) the day the Berlin Wall was built and (2) the day it fell. Collect their liveliest recollections in speech bubbles and match name and age of the persons interviewed and their quotations. Now add how you personally experienced (3) the 25th anniversary of the fall of the Wall on 9th November 2014. Prepare your collection for a gallery walk in the classroom (cf. methodology box) to give all of you a vivid picture of the atmosphere at three historical points in time.

2. **Point out** why, according to Schurman, a "historic opportunity to create [...] a more peaceful world" (l. 11) has been missed and **give a summary** of the journalist's inventory.

3. **Examine** how the journalist puts emphasis on his disappointed hopes for the future. Focus on the presentation of facts and the use of stylistic devices.

4. Are Peter Schurman and John Lennon dreamers because they envision a future in which all people live peacefully together in a global democracy instead of waging war in petty* nation-states? **Discuss**.

petty small and of little importance

The Berlin Wall fell 25 years ago this week. People on both sides filled the streets in celebration, cheered on by virtually everyone around the world. For all of us who were alive then, it remains one of the most hopeful historical moments we've ever experienced.

For the previous two generations, people everywhere had lived in fear. In the East, repressive surveillance* states turned neighbor against neighbor. In the West, we lived under [5] the spectre* of nuclear war and spent a huge share of our wealth on our military, at a ter-

surveillance close observation or supervision
spectre shadow

rible social cost. The overarching* conflict between the US and the Soviet Union drove proxy wars* worldwide.

And suddenly, the cause of all this evaporated*. Surely, a bright, new world was at hand.

10 Now that 25 years have passed, it's an appropriate time to take stock*. Have we seized our historic opportunity to create, at last, a more peaceful world?

Sadly, we have not:

By *Wikipedia's* count, the US has engaged in 10 wars since then, and we now live in a surveillance state the East German secret police would have envied.

15 Russia has reasserted regional military dominance, annexing Crimea, threatening other parts of Ukraine, and re-conquering Chechnya.

The Middle East is a boiling cauldron* of warfare, much of it touched off* by the American invasions of Iraq in 1991 and 2003.

China is building a potentially formidable Navy and picking fights with its neighbors.

20 How can it be that we've made so little progress, following such a breakthrough?

As citizens, we largely left the job of converting the end of the Cold War into a lasting peace in the hands of our national governments. We had little alternative at first: in 1989, the Internet had not yet been widely adopted, so people worldwide had no way to band together at scale*.

25 But now we do. The arrival of the Internet has upended* virtually every major system on earth, revolutionizing our economy and breathing new life into grassroots* politics.

Yet our governance structures remain stubbornly anachronistic*. And they're failing us, not only on the great question of war or peace, but also on many other front-burner* issues today, including global warming, economic inequality, disease response, immigra-
30 tion, human trafficking, and financial crimes.

Although we seldom consider it, one key factor that ties all these failures together is our fragmented system of nation-states, separated by militarized borders.

As the challenges we face grow more urgent, and our national governments' failure to address them more glaring*, the time has come to question this model: whether separate
35 nation-states are still serving us, or whether we can now do better.

Obviously, this is a very big question, and it can quickly conjure images of starry-eyed idealism and John Lennon* songs. But there are practical reasons why it merits serious consideration.

War and peace are just the most obvious of these. Wars typically occur between separate
40 nations. Borders are conceived as safety perimeters*, yet they often contribute to the instability that drives armed conflict. [...]

overarching encompassing
proxy war a war brought about by a major power that does not itself participate (*Stellvertreterkrieg*)
to evaporate to disappear
to take stock to check, to review the situation

cauldron a large pot
to touch off to trigger

at scale considerably, on a large scale
to upend [ʌpˈɛnd] to affect drastically, to upturn, to radically alter
grassroots involving the common people as constituting a fundamental political group
anachronistic antiquated, out-of-date, old-fashioned
front-burner top priority
glaring obvious
John Lennon (born in Liverpool, UK, in 1940, assassinated in NYC in 1980) English singer, songwriter and co-founder of *The Beatles*, cf. the lyrics to his song "Imagine" (1971)
perimeter [pəˈrɪmɪtər] any boundary around something

The fall of the Berlin Wall in 1989

feasible possible

hairy difficult, problematic
audacious [ɔ'deɪʃəs] bold, fearless

The European Union demonstrates a way forward: eliminating militarized borders, and expanding the safety perimeter to include everyone. Yes, everyone – holding criminals, including dictators and terrorists, accountable to the law.

Expanding on best features of the EU model, we could create a single, global democracy. ⁴⁵ [...] Emerging technology can make a global democracy feasible* [...] [although] big challenges remain, notably anonymity, unique voting accounts, and the digital divide, but all of these can be solved with time and commitment. Meanwhile, we can begin the conversation about a global democracy.

What policies would a global democracy produce? There's a lot of reassuring interna- ⁵⁰ tional poll data showing that, while not all mainstream American values are shared worldwide, most are. It appears that people around the world are more likely to agree on the big questions than the actions of certain leaders would suggest. [...]

What if we also had an exciting, positive vision for our future? A big, hairy*, audacious* goal. How about this one: a single, global democracy, within our lifetimes. ⁵⁵

Peter Schurman, "25 Years after Berlin, Do We Still Need Walls?", *The Huffington Post*, 8 November 2014 [08.01.2015]

ZOOM IN: Methodology

During a **gallery walk**, students explore multiple texts or images that are displayed 'gallery-style' (e.g. on walls or tables), enabling them to disperse around the room or to cluster around a particular exhibit. Thus, students can share their work with their peers, examine material in a largely undisturbed fashion and, among themselves, respond to the collection of quotations or pictures. After a few minutes of touring the room, when they are seated again, the students are asked to talk about their personal impressions and about knowledge gained from what they have seen.

M6 # Googling Things

Joshua Ferris

At the beginning of Ferris's novel, Paul O'Rourke, New York City dentist and Red Sox fan, is a man out of touch with modern life. His receptionist and girlfriend Connie, however, is new-media literate.

1. Before reading the excerpt, do some research on *Wikipedia, About.com, IMDb*, the *Zagat* guide, *Time Out New York, Tumblr*, the *New York Times*, and *People* magazine. What do they all have in common? Do you personally resort to any of them? Which search engine did you use to 'google' them, and why did you choose this one?

ZOOM IN: Terminology

A **proprietary eponym** is a trademark of a successful product that refers to the generic class of objects over and above the specific brand itself, e.g. 'kleenex' is used to describe many types of facial tissue, 'to google' stands for the process of searching for information on the Internet.

2. ›› **Outline** a typical evening out at a restaurant with his girlfriend, as presented by the narrator.

3. ›› **Characterise** the narrator and his attitude towards Connie and the new media.

4. ›› **Explain** the term "me-machine" in this context.

5. ›› Do we really always need to have an electronic tool in our hands that connects us to the Internet, our games or our social networks? **Evaluate** situations like those presented in the text and in the photograph.

Joshua Ferris (born in Danville, U.S., in 1974)

Connie was a big one for Googling things. It helped out enormously with all sorts of crises and brought relief to the most pressing concerns. At a restaurant, the two of us would momentarily forget the difference between rigatoni and penne, and she would Google "difference between rigatoni and penne" and provide us the answer. We no longer had to
5 listen to the idiosyncratic* replies of the waitstaff on the differences between rigatoni and penne, which were always so full of human approximations* and stabs* at essences*. We had hard definitions straight from the me-machine. Or while we were drinking our wine, I might ask Connie, who knew more about wine than I did, "Do white wines need time to breathe like red wines?" She wouldn't know the answer, or had known it at one time but
10 had forgotten it and now needed to know it again very badly, so she'd look it up right then and there, at the dinner table, while I waited, and learn not only about aeration* effects on white wines but also quite a lot about grapes, tannins, and oxidation techniques – random snippets* of which, with her eyes cast down on the phone, she would share with me across the table, distractedly and never coherently. She'd also forget who starred in what,
15 who sang this or that, and if so-and-so was still dating so-and-so, and for those things, too, she'd abandon our conversation to secure the answer. She no longer lived in a world of speculation or recall and would take nothing on faith when the facts were but a few clicks away. It drove me nuts. I was sick to death of having as my dinner companions *Wikipedia, About.com, IMDb,* the *Zagat* guide, *Time Out New York,* a hundred *Tumblrs,* the *New York*
20 *Times,* and *People* magazine. Was there not some strange forgotten pleasure in reveling in our ignorance? Couldn't we just be wrong? We fought about that goddamn me-machine more than we fought about where to go and what to do, sex and its frequency, my so-called addiction to the Red Sox, and a million other things combined. (With the exception of kids.
25 We fought most about kids.) I'd had enough and would say things like "The moon is really just a weak star" or "Flour tortillas have ganja* in them" or "My favorite Sean Penn movie is *Forrest Gump*" and then really dig in until she'd
30 Google it and waggle the screen before my eyes as if the thing itself were saying *na na na na na,* and I'd say, "Tom Hanks my ass! It was Sean Penn!" and she'd say, "It's right fucking here, look! Tom Hanks," and I'd say, "I can't believe
35 you needed the Internet for that!" and the night would descend from there.

She sat down and Googled the passage. It returned no exact matches.

Joshua Ferris, *To Rise Again at a Decent Hour*, Viking, London 2014, pp. 70/71, © Joshua Ferris, 2014, reproduced by permission of Penguin Books Ltd.

idiosyncratic characteristic of a specific person
approximation guess
stab attempt, try
essence the most important aspect of something

aeration [ɛəˈreɪʃən] the passing of air through liquid
snippet a small bit

ganja [ˈɡændʒə] marijuana [mæriˈwaːnə]

M7   Social Media and the Loss of Privacy

Modern personal technology (e. g. smartphones, tablets or computers) has not only given us permanent access to information but also the ability to connect with people on the other side of the planet at the touch of a finger. The chart below, based on a survey presented by *Microsoft* at the World Economic Forum in Davos in January 2015, shows how people rate the effect that this technology has on different aspects of their life.

1. >> **Describe** the findings of the survey as presented in the chart.

2. >> Then read the text posted by the administrator of *iCare Consulting*. **Compare** the view that he holds on the correlation between social media and the loss of privacy with the findings of the survey.

3. >> In a class project, prepare to create a bar chart (*Säulendiagramm*) like the one below (cf. skills box). Before doing so, find out which social media you use and how many hours per day you use them. The real work begins now: agree on at least four aspects of life that are affected by your frequent use of these social media. Conduct a little survey in class on whether their effects are positive or negative, and insert the findings in your class chart (aspects/criteria in the middle, negative impact on the left, positive impact on the right). **Evaluate** the results in comparison with those of the *Microsoft* chart.

ZOOM IN: Skills

Creating a Bar Chart

Bar charts can be used to show how something changes over time or to compare items. They have an x-axis (horizontal) and a y-axis (vertical). Typically, the x-axis has numbers for what is being measured. The y-axis, by contrast, has numbers for the amount of what is being measured.

You can easily create such charts without any knowledge of EXCEL software. Just use square paper or one of many simple electronic training programs (e. g. Learning with *NCES*: http://nces.ed.gov/nceskids/ → Graph).

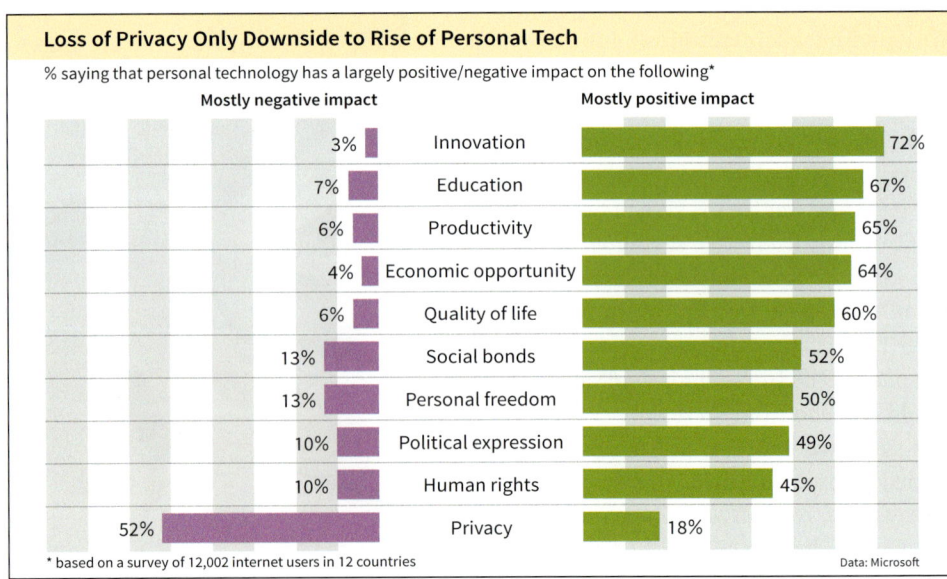

Loss of Privacy Only Downside to Rise of Personal Tech

% saying that personal technology has a largely positive/negative impact on the following*

Mostly negative impact		Mostly positive impact
3%	Innovation	72%
7%	Education	67%
6%	Productivity	65%
4%	Economic opportunity	64%
6%	Quality of life	60%
13%	Social bonds	52%
13%	Personal freedom	50%
10%	Political expression	49%
10%	Human rights	45%
52%	Privacy	18%

* based on a survey of 12,002 internet users in 12 countries   Data: Microsoft

Shaping the Future: Drivers of Global Change **21**

Most of us are connected to one social network or another. For some, it is a necessity and for many others, a great source of income. Should it then come as a surprise that it is also one of the worst breaches of privacy* ever invented? We are ready to unveil* information that we would never share in public to an online audience so large that we may not even
5 estimate* its size. Participation in social media networks leads to a loss of personal information on a scale not previously thought possible before. Plagued with advertisers stealing user information, these networks restrict what can't be shared and give anybody the power to report what their friends are doing at any time. Social media has an important impact on society due to the rampant* abuse of personal information and the loss of pri-
10 vacy.

Whenever a user writes a post, shares a photo or likes a product's page, that user is sending a very large amount of data to everyone who is on his/her friends list, and to many agencies that aren't. These agencies comprise advertisers, marketing analysts, other social researchers and salesmen. The information obtained can then potentially be shared
15 with any number of advertising, spamming and marketing firms. [...]

Not only is social media a means to steal personal information, it is also a way to spread gossip, harmful misinformation, and further abuse. There is no way to really check what is happening in a photo or video, except through user voting and reports. This means that if a humiliating* photo taken at a party is posted, the individuals in the photo have no
20 knowledge that their reputation is being hurt. They will likely not find out until it has

a breach of privacy *here:* the breaking of the moral and legal code of freedom in relation to personal privacy as a result of unauthorised intrusion or distribution of information
to unveil to reveal
to estimate to judge, to assess approximately the significance of something
rampant widespread

to humiliate to make someone feel very ashamed, humble, or foolish

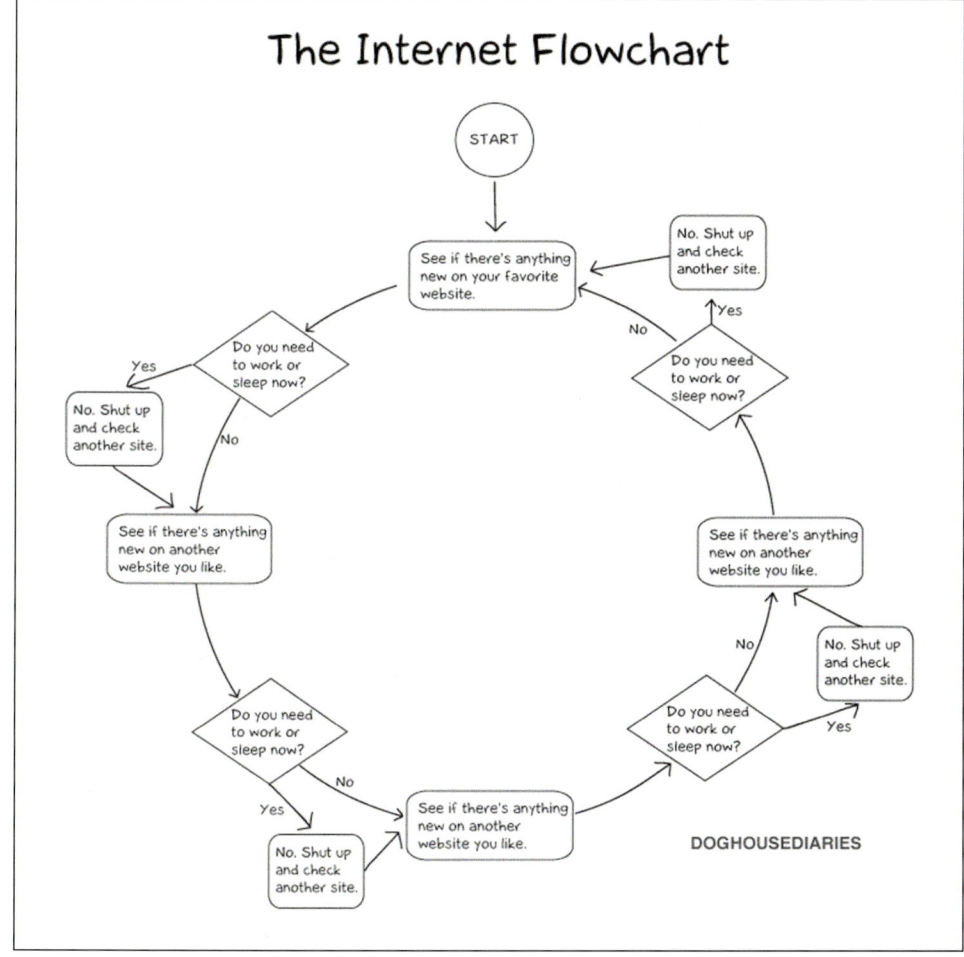

http://thedoghousediaries.com/4432 [30.05.2015]

reached an enormous audience and has harmed their reputation badly. Employers have recently started checking their employees' and prospective employees' Facebook pages for opinions, habits and other subjects that could make them reconsider hiring or continued employment. This means that personal data leaks* are all the more dangerous. Employ- 25 ers looking through their employee's pages or data also has a negative impact as they will have access to the most intimate personal data, what their friends are like and what kind of person they're hiring or have hired. Employees can and will post what they think of their jobs, co-workers and bosses, which may get some more expressive employees fired for their opinions. Not only are employees responsible for keeping their opinions out of their statuses, they are also judged by who they are friends with, needing to clean up or 30 delete friends' comments and posts on their pages.

The loss of privacy is a rising issue among web rights activists as more and more users sign up to share their lives with the world. If a major exploit* is ever found that allowed anyone to see anything posted or otherwise told on any media site, it would have huge repercussions* for both the users and the network's good status. Measures must be taken 35 by social media developers for their users' sakes to stop the misuse of private information, and to take action against the posting of media containing non-consenting individuals and their own carelessness in handling user data. Privacy is being thrown out the window along with inhibition* against sharing even the most private things, which is leading to a whole market based on user data. The loss of privacy is affecting users in myriads* of 40 ways with self-confessions, private information theft and the scrutinizing* eye of their peers reporting all that they do. The participation in social media comes at a very high price. With privacy shriveling at a rapid pace with no signs of stopping, at what point will we be putting it in museums along with the remnants* of our individuality?

Admin, "Social Media and the Loss of Privacy", www.icareconsulting.com, 06.10.2011 [30.05.2015]

leak *here:* escape of information

exploit a bold or daring feat

repercussion consequence

inhibition reservation, something that forbids or restricts
a myriad ['mɪrɪəd] **of** a very large number of things
to scrutinize ['skruːtnaɪz] to examine carefully, mostly in a critical way
remnants the part of something that is left when the rest has gone

---

ZOOM IN: People

Jaron Lanier (born in New York, U.S., in 1960) is a computer philosophy writer, computer scientist and composer of classical music. In 2010, Lanier was nominated in the *TIME 100* list of most influential people. In 2014, he received the Peace Prize awarded by the German Book Trade as "a true pioneer in the digital world – one who has always recognized the inherent risks contained in this new world with regard to each individual's right to shape his or her own life". (www.friedenspreis-des-deutschen-buchhandels.de [30.05.2015])

M8 High-tech Peace Will Need a New Kind of Humanism

Jaron Lanier

The following text is an excerpt from Jaron Lanier's acceptance speech, delivered in Frankfurt on 12 October 2014.

 1. Read the information about Lanier, the title of his speech and the words listed in the cloud. Thereafter, guess what this part of the speech will be dealing with. Bear

in mind that the font sizes of words in a cloud indicate their importance or occurrence frequency.

2. Now read the tasks you are expected to fulfil, then scan the text for information required to fulfil them. Extract and retain this information, either by underlining, making notes in the margin, or making notes in your notebook. Visualise your results (cf. skills pages).

3. **Outline** Lanier's attitude towards advanced digital technology and **point out** what makes him call for a new form of humanism in a humanistic society.

4. **Examine** how Lanier attempts to convince his listeners of the necessity to believe in human specialness. Focus on his line of argument and use of rhetorical devices.

5. Artificial intelligence (AI) is the branch of computer science concerned with making computers behave like humans. Referring to the relevant excerpt of the speech, **assess** the potential benefits and detriments of AI.

Sometimes I wonder if younger people in the developed world, facing the inevitable onslaught* of aging demographics, are subconsciously using
5 the shift to digital technology as a way to avoid being crushed by obligations to an excess of elders. Most parts of the developed world are facing this type of inverted* demo-
10 graphic cataclysm* in the coming decades. Maybe it's proper for young people to seek shelter, but if so, the problem is that they too will become old and needy someday, for that is
15 the human condition.

onslaught a fierce attack

inverted turned upside down
cataclysm [ˈkætəˌklɪzəm] catastrophe

"Artificial intelligence is when you get a college degree, but you're still stupid when you graduate."

stale boring, unoriginal
gerontocracy
[ˌdʒɛrənˈtɒkrəsi] a form
of social organisation in
which a group of old
people dominates

to allocate to apportion
for a specific purpose

grace *here:* favour,
blessing, *Gnade*; a
reference to a poetry
collection by Richard
Brautigan called *All
Watched Over by
Machines of Loving Grace*
(1967)
purported [pəˈpɔːtɪd]
alleged, said to be true
but not necessarily true

epistemological
[ɪˌpɪstɪməˈlɒdʒɪkəl] (*adj.*)
epistemology (*n.*) the
theory of the nature and
grounds of knowledge
especially with reference
to its limits and validity
bell curve a frequency
curve that resembles the
outline of a bell
austerity *here:* a situation
in which there is not
much money and it is
spent only on things that
are necessary
untenable indefensible,
unsupportable

to leech to drain the
substance of something

Within the tiny elite of billionaires who run the cloud computers, there is a loud, confident belief that technology will make them immortal. Google has funded a large organization to "solve death," for instance. There are many other examples. [...]

The arithmetic is clear. If immortality technology, or at least dramatic life extension technology, starts to work, it would either have to be restricted to the tiniest elite, or else we would have to stop adding children to the world and enter into an infinitely stale* gerontocracy*. I point this out only to reinforce that when it comes to digital technology, what seems radical – what at first seems to be creative destruction – is often actually hyperconservative and infinitely stale and boring once it has a chance to play out. 20

Another popular formulation would have our brains "uploaded" into virtual reality so that we could live forever in software form. This despite the fact that we don't know how brains work. We don't yet know how ideas are represented in neurons. We allocate* billions of dollars on simulating brains even though we don't really know the basic principles as yet. We are treating hopes and beliefs as if they were established science. We are treating computers as religious objects. 25 30

We need to consider whether fantasies of machine grace* are worth maintaining. In resisting the fantasies of artificial intelligence, we can see a new formulation of an old idea that has taken many forms in the past: "Humanism."

The new humanism is a belief in people, as before, but specifically in the form of a rejection of artificial intelligence. This doesn't mean rejecting any particular algorithm or robotic mechanism. Every single purported* artificially intelligent algorithm can be equally well understood as a non-autonomous function that people can use as a tool. 35

The rejection is not based on the irrelevant argument usually put forward about what computers can do or not do, but instead on how people are always needed to perceive the computer in order for it to be real. Yes, an algorithm with cloud big data gathered from millions, *millions* of people, can perform a task. You can see the shallowness of computers on a practical level, because of the dependency on a hidden crowd of anonymous people, or a deeper epistemological* one: Without people, computers are just space heaters making patterns. [...] 40

If we just admitted that people are still needed in order for big data to exist, and if we were willing to lessen our fantasies of artificial intelligence, then we might enjoy a new economic pattern in which the bell curve* would begin to appear in digital economic outcomes, instead of winner-take-all results. That might result in sustainable societies that don't fall prey to austerity*, no matter how good or seemingly "automated" technology gets. 45 50

This idea is controversial, to say the least, and I can't argue it fully in this short statement. It is only an idea to be tested, at any rate, and might very well turn out to be untenable*.

But the key point, the essential position from which we must not compromise, is to recognize that there is a space of alternatives. The pattern we see today is not the only possible pattern, and is not inevitable. 55

Inevitability is an illusion that leeches* freedom away.

The more advanced technology gets, the harder it will be to distinguish between algorithms and corporations. Which is Google today, or Facebook? The distinction is already esoteric in those cases and soon will be for many more corporations. If algorithms can be people, then so will be corporations, as they already are in the USA. What I declare here today is that neither an algorithm nor a corporation should be a person! 60

The new humanism asserts that it is ok to believe that people are special, in the sense that people are something more than machines or algorithms. This proposition can lead to crude mocking arguments in tech circles, and really there's no absolute way to prove it's correct. 65

We believe in ourselves and each other only on faith. It is a more pragmatic faith than the traditional belief in God. It leads to a fairer and more sustainable economy, and better, more accountable technology designs, for instance. (Believing in people is compatible with any belief or lack of belief in God.)

70 To some techies, a belief in the specialness of people can sound sentimental or religious, and they hate that. But without believing in human specialness, how can a humanistic society be sought?

May I suggest that technologists at least try to pretend to believe in human specialness to see how it feels?

Jaron Lanier, "High-tech Peace Will Need a New Kind of Humanism", www.friedenspreis-des-deutschen-buchhandels.de, 12.10.2014 [30.05.2015]

M 9 You'd Never Guess Your 'Friend' Doesn't Have a Heartbeat

M 9a Roboter-Propaganda

Frank Seibert

 1. The photo below shows a receptionist of *Henn-na Hotel* in Nagasaki prefecture, whose reception desk is manned* by three (out of a total of ten) 'Actroid' robots. These human-shaped robots look like life-size dolls, are multilingual, maintain eye contact and blink. Talk about the photo with a partner. How does it make you feel?

to man to be present to operate something

2. An American pen pal of yours mentions in an e-mail that more and more friends are contacting him via *Twitter* who seem to have the same interests and tastes as himself and that he is very happy about all the concrete tips they offer as to what flashy outfits to buy or what music events to attend. As chance would have it, you have just read a news item in *Neon* on robots surfing the Internet, pretending to be genuine users. Respond to your pen pal by e-mail, mediating that information in English.

 3. Against the backdrop of what the news item tells you about fake accounts with fake profiles for advertising purposes, will you personally go on using social media such as *Twitter*, *Facebook* or *WhatsApp*, or will you quit? **Discuss** with a partner.

ZOOM IN: Skills

Translation vs. mediation

A **translation** is a detailed and exact stylistic equivalent of the original text or speech in a different language.

In a **mediation**, however, you communicate the gist of a source text or speech in the target language analogously and in a manner that is audience-oriented. This implies that you will occasionally need to make necessary alterations or add further explanations while not affecting the main point at issue.

Examine the example given in this table. The target text format of this mediation task is that of an e-mail among pen pals, and the person addressed is a young American adult.

Original text	Translation	Mediation
Das US-Verteidigungsministerium suchte zum Beispiel in einer öffentlichen Ausschreibung eine Firma, die eine Bot-Armee mit Hunderten Fake-Identitäten entwickelt. Die Armee gab zu, dass es ihr Ziel sei, die Meinung im Netz zu beeinflussen.	In a public tender the US Department of Defense, for example, ran a search for a company that would engineer an army of bots with hundreds of fake identities. The US Army admitted that it was their aim to influence opinions on the net.	I'll give you an example: Your country's Department of Defense has just tried to have loads of fake-identity bots built because they wanted to manipulate our opinions as net users.

---

austauschen to exchange
teilnehmen (an) to participate (in)
sich zoffen to have a row

erstellen to create
pflegen to maintain
Profilbild profile picture
Lebenslauf *curriculum vitae* (Latin) [kəˌrɪkjʊləmˈviː.taɪ]
mutmaßlich allegedly [əˈlɛdʒd]
falsch fake
einordnen to codify
Kontrolleur supervisor
öffentliche Ausschreibung public tender

Im Netz tauschen wir Meinungen aus*. An der Debatte nehmen aber längst nicht nur Menschen teil*.

Wer im Netz Streit sucht, bekommt ihn auch. Aber wer zofft sich* da eigentlich mit wem? Menschen natürlich und, da sind sich Social-Media-Experten und Wissenschaftler sicher, immer mehr Roboter. Viele der Posts werden mittlerweile von Bots geschrieben – Programmen, die autonom Accounts in sozialen Netzwerken erstellen* und pflegen* können – mit authentisch wirkendem Profilbild*, Lebenslauf* und Interessen. Twitter gab 2014 an, dass etwa 24 Millionen seiner Nutzer – neun Prozent – mutmaßlich* Bots sind, Facebook geht gar von bis zu 137 Millionen falschen* Profilen aus. Die Programme können Meinungen erkennen, einordnen* – und genau die Antwort geben, die im Interesse des Bot-Kontrolleurs* ist. Die Bots stellen eine neue Möglichkeit für Konzerne, Lobbygruppen und Regierungen dar, Werbung zu machen und Einfluss auf die öffentliche Meinung zu nehmen. Das US-Verteidigungsministerium suchte zum Beispiel in einer öffentlichen Ausschreibung* eine Firma, die eine Bot-Armee mit Hunderten Fake-Identitäten entwickelt. Die Armee gab zu, dass es ihr Ziel sei, die Meinung im Netz zu beeinflussen.

Frank Seibert, „Roboter-Propaganda", *NEON*, April 2015, S. 28

---

to eavesdrop to listen secretly to the private conversation of others

M 9b Child Advocates Mobilize to Stop Mattel's Eavesdropping 'Hello Barbie'

1. **Point out** why child advocates are trying to stop the production of Mattel's latest Barbie doll.

2. **Explain** why a doll like 'Hello Barbie' could pose a threat to a child's healthy development.

3. **Comment** on Mattel's goal to make the child and 'Hello Barbie' "become like the best of friends".

Campaign for a Commercial-Free Childhood (CCFC) is demanding that toymaker Mattel halt marketing and
5 production of its planned 'Hello Barbie'. The Wi-Fi-connected doll uses an embedded microphone to record children's voices – and other near-
10 by conversations – before transmitting them over the Internet to cloud servers. Mat-

tel's technology partner ToyTalk then processes the audio with voice-recognition software. During its Toy Fair 2015 product demonstration, Mattel said it will use this information to
15 "push data" back to children through Barbie's built-in speaker.

"Kids using 'Hello Barbie' aren't only talking to a doll, they are talking directly to a toy conglomerate* whose only interest in them is financial," said Dr. Susan Linn, CCFC's Executive Director. "It's creepy – and creates a host* of dangers for children and families."
Angela Campbell, JD, Georgetown University Law Professor and Faculty Advisor to the
20 school's Center on Privacy and Technology, said, "If I had a young child, I would be very concerned that my child's intimate conversations with her doll were being recorded and analyzed. In Mattel's demo, Barbie asks many questions that would elicit* a great deal of information about a child, her interests, and her family. This information could be of great value to advertisers and be used to market unfairly to children."
25 The companies say that they will obtain parental permission to capture* a child's voice, but that won't necessarily protect children from exploitation. For example, ToyTalk's current privacy policy states:

We may use, store, process and transcribe Recordings in order to provide and maintain the Service, to perform, test or improve speech recognition technology and artificial intel-
30 ligence algorithms, or for other research and development and data analysis purposes.

A Mattel spokeswoman claims the toy will "deepen that relationship girls have with [Barbie]." Over time, she says, the goal is for the child and 'Hello Barbie' to "become like the best of friends."

"Computer algorithms can't replace – and should not displace – the nuanced responsive-
35 ness* of caring people interacting with one another," according to pediatrician* Dipesh Navsaria, MPH, MD, assistant professor at the University of Wisconsin School of Medicine and Public Health. "Children's well-being and healthy development demand relationships and conversations with *real* people and *real* friends. Children do not need commercially manufactured messages – artificially created after listening in on anyone within
40 range of Mattel's microphones."

Dr. Linn added, "'Hello Barbie' not only discourages the kind of creative play essential for learning and development, it ensures that Mattel – not the child – is driving the play."

Josh Golin, "Child Advocates Mobilize to Stop Mattel's Eavesdropping 'Hello Barbie'", www.commercialfreechildhood.org, 10.03.2015 [30.05.2015]

---

conglomerate a corporation made up of a number of different companies that operate in diversified fields
host a great number

to elicit to draw out

to capture *here:* to transfer into a computer

responsiveness the quality of reacting quickly, which involves responding with emotion to people and events
p(a)ediatrician [ˌpiːdiəˈtrɪʃən] a specialist in the care of infants, children, and adolescents

---

4. ⟩ **Compare** the two texts (M 9a and M 9b) and **point out** similarities.

5. ⟩ Revise what you have learned so far about some of the drivers of global change.
Discuss which of these drivers is the most powerful one, i. e. the one that has altered the reality of life most radically.

M 1
The 12 Terrifying Ways Researchers Think Human Civilisation Is Most Likely to End

Jon Stone

In February 2015, scientists from the *Global Challenges Foundation* published a compilation of twelve ways human civilisation is most likely to end. In their study, they define a civilisation collapse as a "drastic decrease in human population size and political/economic/social complexity, globally and for an extended time."

1. Make an educated guess as to which global threats will be considered the most terrifying in this study. You may use the photographs below as stimuli.

2. **Describe** the twelve global risks and their probable impact on human civilisation, as summarised by Jon Stone from *The Independent*.

3. The scientific study classifies these risks into four categories: current risks, exogenic* risks, emerging risks and global policy risks. Decide which category each of the twelve risks belongs to, and **explain** why.

4. Make your personal ranking list by arranging the twelve global challenges in order of their risk potential. Start with what threatens you most. Feel free to add risks that, in your opinion, may also lead to a global collapse. **Justify** your decision.

exogenic derived or originating externally; *antonym:* **endogenic** derived or originating internally

Extreme climate change

The likelihood of global coordination to stop climate change is seen by the authors of the study as the biggest controllable factor in whether the environmental catastrophe can be prevented. 5

They also warn that the impact of climate change could be strongest in the poorest countries and that mass deaths from famines* and huge migration trends could 10 cause major global instability.

Nuclear war

famine ['fæmɪn] a situation in which many people do not have enough food to eat **to concede** to admit usually in an unwilling way

deliberate done or decided after careful thought

While the researchers concede* that a nuclear war is less likely than in the previous century, they say that evidence suggests 15 "the potential for deliberate* or accidental nuclear conflict has not been removed".

The biggest fact which they say would influence whether one happens would be how relations between future and current 20 nuclear powers develop.

Global pandemic*

"There are grounds for suspecting that such a high impact epidemic is more prob-
25 able than usually assumed," the research-
ers believe.

The ability of the world's medical systems to respond to a pandemic is important in preventing a catastrophe, researchers say
30 – but the biggest threat is simply whether there is an uncontrollable infectious dis-
ease out there or not.

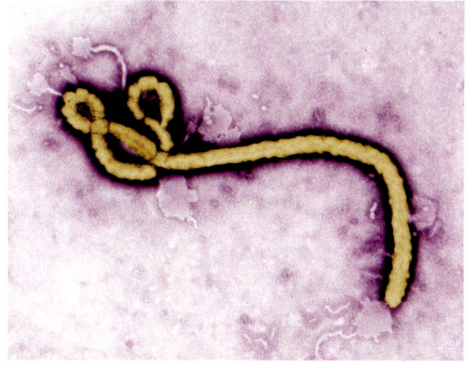

pandemic a worldwide epidemic of infectious disease

Major asteroid impact

An asteroid impact larger than 5km in size would destroy an area the size of the Nether-
35 lands, the researchers warn. They say these events happen every 20m* years.

"Should an impact occur, the main destruction will not be from the initial impact, but from the clouds of dust projected into the upper atmosphere," the study warns.

"The damage from such an 'impact winter' could affect the climate, damage the bio-
sphere, affect food supplies, and create political instability."

m one million

40 Supervolcano

Like an asteroid impact, the greatest threat from a super-volcano is a global dust-cloud that would block the sun's rays and cause a global winter. "The effect [of historic erup-
45 tions] could be best compared with that of a nuclear war," the researchers state.

The ability to stop damage depends on the ability of nations to coordinate and limit the damage they cause.

50 Ecological catastrophe

Humanity either has to conserve the eco-
system, or hope that civilisation is not de-
pendent on it.

"Species extinction* is now far faster than
55 the historic rate," the study warns. Humanity must develop sustainable economies in order to survive this one.

extinction the state or situation that results when something (such as a plant or animal species) has died out completely

Global system collapse

"The world economic and political system is made up of many actors with many objectives
60 and many links between them," the study warns. "Such intricate*, interconnected systems are subject to unexpected system-wide failures caused by the structure of the network".

Economic collapse could lead to social chaos, civil unrest and a breakdown in law and order.

intricate ['ɪntrɪkɪt] difficult to resolve or analyse

65 Synthetic biology

The scientists are worried that someone will intentionally build an "engineered pathogen*" to wipe out the human race.

"Attempts at regulation or self-regulation
70 are currently in their infancy, and may not develop as fast as research does," they warn.

pathogen ['pæθədʒɛn] something (such as a type of bacteria or a virus) that causes disease

nanotechnology the science of working with atoms and molecules to build devices (such as robots) that are extremely small
proponent a person who argues for or supports something
to tout to attempt to persuade someone of the merits of something
novel new and different from what has been known before
to boost to increase the force, power or amount

AI artificial intelligence
plethora [ˈplɛθərə] a very large amount
entity something that has a separate and distinct existence and objective or conceptual reality
twist *here:* a sudden change in approach or meaning
overlord a person who has power over a large number of people
governance the way that a company, a city, a country, etc. is controlled by the people who run it

Nanotechnology*

Nanotechnology's proponents* tout* it as a way to solve problems, but the researchers believe it could present serious problems.

"[Nanotechnology] could lead to the easy construction of large arsenals of conventional or 75 more novel* weapons made possible by atomically precise manufacturing," they warn, before adding: "Of particular relevance is whether nanotechnology allows the construction of nuclear bombs."

Artificial intelligence

The researchers believe that forms of "extreme" arti- 80 ficial intelligence "could not be easily controlled" and would "probably act to boost* their own intelligence and acquire maximal resources".

Rather spookily, they say one of the key factors in our survival is whether "there will be a single domi- 85 nant AI* or a plethora* of entities*".

In a bit of a twist*, they concede that a powerful artificial intelligence might make solving all the other risks in the report much easier. All hail our new computer overlords*? 90

Future bad global governance*

The message here is that if politicians don't come up with solutions to the other problems in the list, they are a risk in and of themselves.

"There are two main divisions in governance disas- 95 ters: failing to solve major solvable problems, and actively causing worse outcomes," the study explains.

Uncertain risks

Finally, the researchers warn of "unknown unknowns" and call for "extensive research" 100 into "unknown risks and their probabilities".

"One resolution to the Fermi paradox – the apparent absence of alien life in the galaxy – is that intelligent life destroys itself before it can begin to expand into the galaxy." It's all very cheery.

Jon Stone, "The 12 Terrifying Ways Researchers Think Human Civilisation Is Most Likely to End", www.independent. co.uk, 15.02.2015 [30.05.2015]

ZOOM IN: Terminology

The Fermi Paradox seeks to answer the question of where the aliens are. Given that our globe is part of a young planetary system compared to the rest of the universe and that interstellar travel might be fairly easy to achieve, the theory says that we should already have been colonised, or at least been visited by aliens. However, Enrico Fermi, an Italian physicist (1901–1954), saw no evidence of this, nor of signs of intelligence elsewhere in our galaxy.

In the decades since, the possible implications of this simple paradox have led extra-terrestrial researchers to form multiple and frequently strange ideas and hypotheses.

 5. Our galaxy should be teeming with civilisations, but where are they? What is blocking galactic civilisation? SETI, the Search for Extra-terrestrial Intelligence, is an institute that conducts exploratory research, seeking evidence of life in the universe by looking for some signature of its technology (www.seti.org). Do some research into their work, then prepare a five-minute talk and give it in class.

M2 The Onslaught of the Ebola Virus

M2a David Quammen on Ebola, Globalization and Viral Epidemics

Lara Salahi

David Quammen is an American science, nature and travel writer, the author of numerous fiction and nonfiction books and a regular contributor to *National Geographic* magazine.

onslaught a sudden and severe onset of trouble

1. Before reading, do some research on the latest Ebola outbreak. Then, against the backdrop of what you know about the risks of globalization (cf. M1), ponder the connection between viral epidemics and globalization.

2. After reading, **summarise** Quammen's views on global preparedness for viral outbreaks and on the uneasy relationship between public health and civil liberties.

3. **Analyse** how Quammen uses language and style to convince the readers of *Ebola Deeply (ED)* of his view.

4. Write a letter to the editor, commenting on Quammen's assessment that Ebola "is not a horror movie thing" (ll. 52) but "the dress rehearsal" for a more viral epidemic to come (l. 17)

ED: Do you expect that more people in the U.S. will be infected with Ebola before we begin to see the virus contained*?

Quammen: I don't expect a conflagration* of the disease in the U.S., but more sparks that will need to be extinguished. A spark landed in Dallas, a spark landed in New York.
5 They've all been extinguished so far, short of causing new outbreaks. The transmission to nurses in Dallas was unexpected and scary for some people. We all wondered, what happened in Dallas [that two nurses were infected as a result of caring for an infected patient]? And how does it happen twice? There has been no secondary spread, which is huge and brings me confidence that the sparks can be contained.
10 I think there will be more sparks, but I'm optimistic they will be kept in check. In the U.S. and elsewhere we badly need to get our protocols for travelers consistent* – whether there should be unrestricted travel to West Africa, whether there should be added screening* and quarantine measures. There should be consistent answers. We also need to know who's in charge of creating these policies – whether it's the federal, state or local govern-
15 ments.
We need to put out the conflagration in West Africa. I've said this before: I don't think that Ebola is a pandemic, but it's the dress rehearsal* for the next big one. Our response to Ebola thus far suggests that we're not ready. I believe the next big one will be a respiratory disease* and we're not ready.
20 *ED:* A number of states have proposed implementing mandatory* 21-day self-quarantine measures to their residents returning from regions in West Africa. Do you think the practice will effectively manage the spread of the virus?

to contain *here:* to keep within limits
conflagration a large destructive fire, an inferno

consistent coherent and uniform
screening testing persons, *here* in order to identify symptoms of a contagious disease

dress rehearsal *Generalprobe*
respiratory disease *Atemwegserkrankung*
mandatory obligatory

to omit to leave out
sound bite short catchy statement replayed by reporters

to facilitate to help forward

misallocation assigning resources wrongly or inappropriately

unduly (1) excessively; (2) unjustifiably

Quammen: We're coming into an era when there will be conflict between public health and civil liberties. I agree that mandatory quarantine is a violation of civil liberties, but we need to talk about it in public.   25

There is a scientific basis to quarantining as a precaution. However, the words that get omitted* in media statements and sound bites* are "probably; as far as we know", that 21-days is enough to see symptoms. Society has some legitimate concerns here [regarding the virus's spread into their community]. I think [returning healthcare workers who are asked to self-quarantine] need to recognize society's concerns here.   30

Our knowledge of Ebola is not experimental science – we know about Ebola from how it has presented in West Africa, but our challenge here is how best to manage its potential spread here. If we do a mandatory quarantine for everybody coming back from West Africa, who's going to be in charge of facilitating* that? We're not ready for that. Is it even possible to quarantine all who return if we wanted to do it? Do we have the resources? I   35 think an argument can be made that there'll be a misallocation* of resources and a false sense of security. [...]

We need to make decisions as a society as to what is right based on consensus by scientific experts and there should be a single policy – which may need to take an act of legislation.   40

ED: Does the slowing spread of the virus in West African countries like Liberia in any way forecast the virus' spread in the U.S.?

Quammen: It is promising because if it's slowing it's headed toward stopping. I don't know if there's a linear correlation between the spread abroad and in the U.S. Most who are infected in West Africa may never have the money to make it to the U.S. That's not to   45 say that it can't infect other people – but demographically, those who've suffered most are the poorest segment in these African countries. [...]

ED: In your opinion, what are some of the top concerns the U.S. faces in treating and managing the spread of Ebola?

Quammen: My top concern is that people fear this virus unduly* because of the   50 misconceptions surrounding its visible symptoms, because they may think it's bloody and causes organs to dissolve. It's a terrible disease but it's not a horror movie thing. That concern spans from people being too scared of Ebola for the wrong reasons.

I think the real concern lies in understanding that this is not the end of an outbreak of this kind – which leads to my second concern. In our urgent response to Ebola, people are   55 going to think that once we solve this problem then we're done. I think once we solve this problem, it will become a pretext for something bigger and more easily spreadable coming next.

Lara Salahi, "David Quammen on Ebola, Globalization and Viral Epidemics", *Ebola Deeply*, 30.10.2014 [16.09.2015]

5. Against the backdrop of what Quammen says about Americans "unduly" fearing the Ebola virus (l. 50), briefly describe Gary Varvel's cartoon and **comment** on its message.

M 2b Why Ebola Is So Dangerous

1. Study the graphics (cf. M 5, skills & vocabulary box). Then **describe** what the Ebola virus is, how and where it spreads, and whom it has affected up to now.

2. After doing further research on Ebola on the World Health Organization's homepage (see Webcode), **explain** what precautions people can take to avoid contracting the disease.

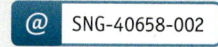
@ SNG-40658-002

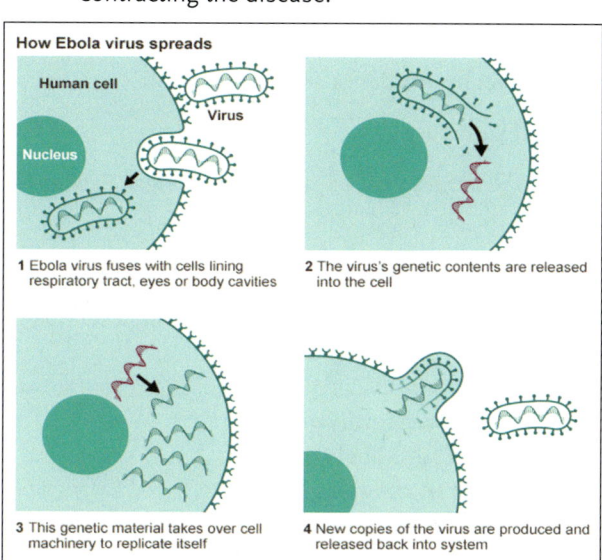

How Ebola virus spreads

Human cell — Virus — Nucleus

1 Ebola virus fuses with cells lining respiratory tract, eyes or body cavities

2 The virus's genetic contents are released into the cell

3 This genetic material takes over cell machinery to replicate itself

4 New copies of the virus are produced and released back into system

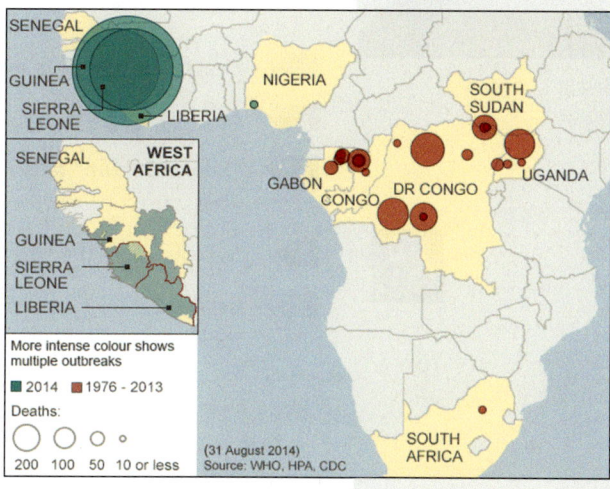

SENEGAL, GUINEA, SIERRA LEONE, LIBERIA, NIGERIA, SOUTH SUDAN, GABON, CONGO, DR CONGO, UGANDA

WEST AFRICA — SENEGAL, GUINEA, SIERRA LEONE, LIBERIA

SOUTH AFRICA

More intense colour shows multiple outbreaks
■ 2014 ■ 1976 - 2013
Deaths: 200 100 50 10 or less
(31 August 2014)
Source: WHO, HPA, CDC

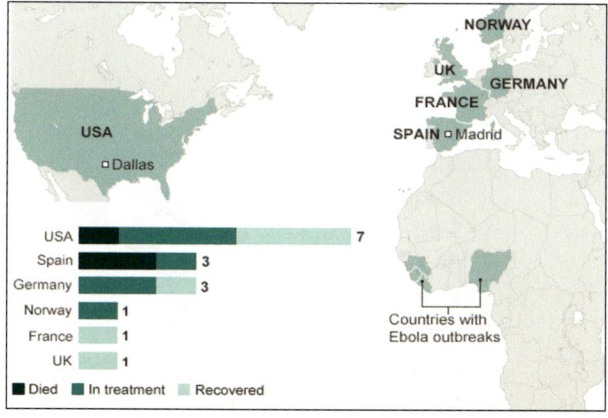

NORWAY, UK, GERMANY, FRANCE, SPAIN □ Madrid, USA □ Dallas

USA	7
Spain	3
Germany	3
Norway	1
France	1
UK	1

Countries with Ebola outbreaks
■ Died ■ In treatment ■ Recovered

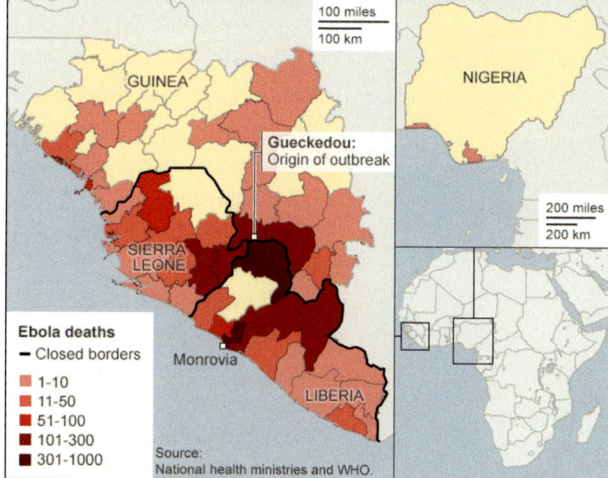

100 miles / 100 km
GUINEA — NIGERIA
Gueckedou: Origin of outbreak
200 miles / 200 km
SIERRA LEONE — Monrovia — LIBERIA

Ebola deaths
– Closed borders
■ 1-10
■ 11-50
■ 51-100
■ 101-300
■ 301-1000
Source: National health ministries and WHO.

ZOOM IN: Vocabulary

contagious highly infectious, transmissible by direct or indirect contact
to contain a disease to keep a disease from spreading (within limits)
to contaminate to make dangerous, dirty, or impure by adding something harmful or undesirable
to contract a disease to become ill, for example by exposure to something contagious
precaution preventive measure
to replicate to duplicate, copy or reproduce
respiratory tract the nose, throat, trachea [trəˈkiːə], bronchi [ˈbrɒŋkaɪ] and lungs
secretion substance such as saliva, mucus, tears, bile, breast milk or a hormone that is secreted

Samuel "Shadow"
Morgan

M 2c Ebola in Town

Samuel "Shadow" Morgan

Ebola has been responsible for thousands of deaths, for fear, panic, disbelief, and anger – and for the catchy dance song "Ebola in Town". The producers behind this music are Samuel "Shadow" Morgan and Edwin "D-12" Tweh, who both spent time as children in refugee camps in Ghana after fleeing the civil war back home in Liberia.

1. First of all, ask yourself what to expect from a dance song about Ebola.

2. After reading the lyrics, give a brief **summary**.

3. "Ebola in Town" falls in the category of the so-called 'awareness songs'. **Explain** why.

4. Now listen to the song and **examine** how the music lines up with the words.

5. **Evaluate** if it is appropriate to use dance floor beats when dealing with a serious topic such as a deadly disease.

Something happen
Something in town
Oh yeah the news
I said something in town
5 Ebola
Ebola in town
Don't touch your friend!
No touching
No eating something
10 It's dangerous!
Ebola
Ebola in town
Don't touch your friend!
No kissing!
15 No eating something
It's dangerous!
I woke up in the morning
I started hearing people dem[1] yelling
"Da what thing happen? What thing happen?
20 Ma peekin'[2] what thing?"
They sit down grab me
They say something in town
Frisky[3]!
That thing that in town it quick to kill
25 That me scary-o[4]
E-B-O-L-A
Ebola. Ebola in town.
I started yelling.
I started running.
30 What place I will go?
I go to Guinea.

I went everywhere.
Ebola. Ebola there.
I'm not going anywhere.
35 I'm right here.
I'm not going nowhere-o.
I'm right here.
I know the medicine.
That distant hugging
40 I said distant shaking
Distant kissing
Don't touch me!
Something in town-oh
Something in town-eh
45 Ebola.
Ebola in town.
It's dangerous-o.
Ebola is very wicked.
It can kill you quick quick.
50 Be careful how you shaking hands-o.
Be careful who you touch.
Ebola is more than HIV/AIDS.
It can kill you quick quick.
It can kill you fast fast.
55 Don't touch your friend.
Don't touch your friend.
I say it will kill you-o.
My pa[5] Jehovah[6]
Please save us from Ebola
60 Nowhere to go
Nowhere to hide
And I ain't[7] come in town

My people, ya'll[8] please take time
Take time before you get that disease
65 Don't overlook it
That thing it quick to kill
Na na na na. Ebola – o.
It's dangerous.
Don't take it for joke
70 My people, I saw it before
It coming too fast
Be on the safe side, you hear me?
Ebola.

If you like the monkey
75 Don't eat the meat[9]
If you like the baboon
I said don't eat the meat
If you like the bat-o
Don't eat the meat
80 Ebola in town.

Samuel "Shadow" Morgan/Edwin "D-12" Tweh, "Ebola in Town", Shadow's Entertainment 2014

---

[1] **dem** them   [2] **ma peekin'** *here:* I'm excited   [3] **frisky** *here:* crazy   [4] **that me scary** that scares me   [5] **pa** father   [6] **Jehovah** (the Hebrew name for) God   [7] **ain't** am not   [8] **ya'll** you all   [9] **meat** bush meat from animals such as chimpanzees, gorillas, fruit bats, monkeys, forest antelope and porcupines is a prized delicacy in much of West Africa but can also be a source of Ebola

M3 The Global Wealth Gap: It's Time to Even It up!

Global wealth is increasingly being concentrated in the hands of a small wealthy elite. In 2014, the richest 1 % of adults in the world owned 48 % of global wealth, leaving just 52 % to be shared between the other 99 % of adults on the planet. Almost all of that 52 % is owned by those included in the richest 20 %, leaving just 5.5 % for the remaining 80 % of people in the world.

(Deborah Hardoon, "Wealth: Having It All and Wanting More", www.oxfam.org, 19.01.2015 [30.05.2015]).

1. What is poverty? Is it simply the lack of money? And why does being poor mean living in a vicious circle? Try to answer these questions with a partner and present your results in the form of a circle chart (cf. skills pages).

2. Have you ever heard of *Oxfam*? Research the non-profit organisation's policy and beliefs and try to find out how they fight poverty.

3. **Outline** why it is "time to even up*", according to *Oxfam* and one of its heads.

to even up to make or become equal

4. With their *Even It Up!* campaign, *Oxfam* invites us to fundraise and donate money that will lift lives for good in some of the world's poorest communities. **Examine** how they proceed to win us over. Focus on composition, language and style.

5. **Discuss** whether fundraising and donating money is an effective means of coping with inequality and poverty.

Extreme inequality is hurting us all – damaging economic growth, fuelling* crime, and squandering* the hopes and ambitions of billions who are trapped at the bottom with no way out.

Such stark inequality is not inevitable – it is the consequence of political and economic
5 choices. With extreme wealth comes power and influence – we're living in a world where the rules are rigged* in favour of the few and at the expense of the many. So while the wealth of the few grows greater, the poorest are left behind.

It doesn't have to be this way – together we can even things up. We can change the rules on tax to make sure the richest pay their fair share. We can demand more spending on

to fuel to stimulate the existence of something
to squander ['skwɒndə] to waste

to rig *here:* to manipulate

10 public health and education to give the poor a fighting chance. We can demand fair wages for everyone. We can make sure the poorest have a voice, and those voices are heard by those in power.

Did you know?

Since the financial crisis the number of billionaires has more than doubled and in that 15 same period at least a million mothers died in childbirth.

Oxfam has calculated that in 2014 the richest 85 people on the planet owned as much as the poorest half of humanity.

Last year the richest 85 people saw their wealth increase by half a million dollars every minute.

20 Seven out of ten people live in countries where the gap between the rich and poor is worse than thirty years ago.

Today there are 16 billionaires in sub-Saharan Africa, alongside the 358 million people living in extreme poverty.

Every year, 100 million people are pushed into poverty because they have to pay for health 25 care.

Without action, it will take 75 years to achieve equal pay between men and women.

The time is now.

30 The world has woken up to the gap between the rich and rest. From Spain to South Africa, and Peru to Pakistan, people are already 35 demanding a world that is fairer than this.

Oxfam International, "It's time to Even It Up!", www.oxfam.org, [30.05.15]

Billionaires who have the same amount of wealth as the poorest half of world's population

Number of billionaires

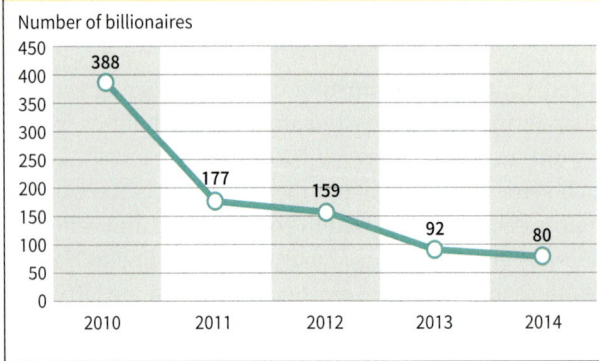

In response to the *Forbes Rich List** published today, which reveals there are now a record 1,826 billionaires in the world worth $7.05 trillion, Nick Bryer, Oxfam's Head of UK Policy, Programs and Campaigns said:

"This is yet more evidence that the very few at the top are coining it in*. At the other end
5 of the scale there are nearly a billion people who go to bed hungry every night. Such extreme inequality should concern us all, not only because it is a moral outrage*, but because it is undermining* growth and creating one of the most significant barriers to ending poverty.

"Economic growth does not inevitably trickle down* to help those at the bottom. Money
10 can be used to buy power and rig rules, regulations and policies, creating this huge void* between the rich and poor and between those who can and cannot access opportunities.

"Unfair tax rules are a perfect example of this. A fairer global tax system, which clamps down* on tax dodging* by corporations and rich individuals, would help to close this gap and tackle the growing problem of inequality."

Oxfam International, "2015 Forbes List exposes income inequality among the 1%, despite highest ever number of billionaires: Oxfam reaction", www.oxfam.org [30.05.2015]

Forbes Rich List *cf.*
terminology box

to coin in to make money rapidly

outrage something that is grossly offensive to morality
to undermine to weaken gradually
to trickle down to be distributed to someone in little bits at a time
void an empty space
to clamp down to impose more strict control
to dodge to avoid

ZOOM IN: Terminology

The **Forbes Rich List** is an annual ranking of the world's wealthiest people, compiled and published by the American business magazine *Forbes* in March. The total net worth of each individual on the list is estimated in US dollars, based on their assets and accounting for debt. Royalty and dictators, whose wealth comes from their positions, are excluded from the list. *Microsoft* founder Bill Gates has topped the list for many years, including 2015.

---

6. Watch a short video clip of the *Even It Up!* campaign on *YouTube* (see Webcode). If necessary, skim the transcript to fill in any gaps in understanding. Then prepare to explain to your classmates why the scope of inequality has got out of control and how, according to *Oxfam*, we can change this.

7. Investigate if there are any non-profit organisations in your town that are committed to bridging the wealth gap. Based on your investigation, write an article for the school magazine, introducing these organisations and describing their local commitment.

SNG-40658-003

M4   We Refugees

Benjamin Zephaniah

1. **Describe** all four photographs (cf. skills & vocabulary box).

2. Do further research on the present situation of refugees all over the world. Then focus on the trouble spot that grieves you most deeply and prepare a five-minute talk about the situation there.

Syrian refugee children standing inside a tent at a refugee camp during snowfall in East Lebanon on 7 January 2015.

Migrants waiting in the port of Lampedusa to board a ferry and be transferred to Sicily on 20 February 2015.

African migrants are sitting atop a perimeter fence round a golf course during an attempt to cross from Morocco into the Spanish enclave of Melilla on 22 October 2014.

South Sudanese civilians fleeing the violence in their country, in the border town of Joda, Sudan, 16 January 2014.

Describing photographs

- Start by introducing the date and the setting of the photograph, e. g. *The photograph dates from …/the scene takes place in a street/on a dirt road/in Lebanon/during the day/at night/in winter.*
- Be as precise as you can when you describe the photograph. Use present progressive to describe what is happening **in** the photograph, adjectives for the appearance of people, adverbs of manner (how?) for their activities, and some 'position' language, for example:

  in the top left(-hand) corner   *at* the top   *in* the top right(-hand) corner
  on the left(-hand) (side)   *in* the middle/centre   *on* the right(-hand) (side)
  in the bottom left(-hand) corner   *at* the bottom   *in* the bottom right(-hand) corner
  in the foreground/background
  of the photograph.

- Express your opinion on the content and message of the photograph, for example: *In my opinion, …/As I see it, …/I suppose/believe/think/guess …*

Useful words and expressions for describing the photographs above

1. **Holzpalette** wooden pallet • **(Zelt-)Plane** tarp(aulin) • **bunt gekleidet** wearing pied clothing • **vor der Kamera posen** to pose in front of the camera
2. **Kai** quay, waterfront • **eingezäunt** fenced in • **mittellos festsitzen** to be stranded without any money • **Kapuzenpulli** hoodie • **eingeschüchtert** intimidated • **erschöpft** exhausted • **Sicherheitskräfte** security forces
3. **Golfplatz** golf course • **den Schläger schwingen** to swing one's club • **Grenzzaun aus Maschendraht** wire-mesh border • perimeter fence • **ungestört** undisturbed • **teilnahmslos** apathetic, unresponsive
4. **auf der Flucht** on the run • **Hab und Gut** one's belongings • **Rückenansicht** rear view • **rastlos** unresting • **heimatlos** displaced

---

Benjamin Zephaniah is a British-Jamaican Rastafarian poet, who was included in *The Times* list of Britain's top 50 post-war writers in 2008.

3. ▷ **Describe** the fate of the speaker and **state** the message he conveys to us, his audience.

4. ▷ **Illustrate** how the poet makes use of stylistic devices to convey his feelings about having to leave his native country.

5. ▷ Against the backdrop of your work on global trouble spots (cf. task 2), **assess** the meaning of the speaker's statement that "Nobody's here without a struggle" (l. 47).

Benjamin Zephaniah (born in Birmingham, UK, in 1958)

We Refugees

I come from a musical place
Where they shoot me for my song
And my brother has been tortured
By my brother in my land.

5 I come from a beautiful place
Where they hate my shade of skin
They don't like the way I pray
And they ban free poetry.

I come from a beautiful place
10 Where girls cannot go to school
There you are told what to believe
And even young boys must grow beards.

I come from a great old forest
I think it is now a field
15 And the people I once knew
Are not there now.

We can all be refugees
Nobody is safe,
All it takes is a mad leader
20 Or no rain to bring forth food,
We can all be refugees
We can all be told to go,
We can be hated by someone
For being someone.

25 I come from a beautiful place
Where the valley floods each year
And each year the hurricane tells us
That we must keep moving on.

I come from an ancient place
30 All my family were born there
And I would like to go there
But I really want to live.

I come from a sunny, sandy place
Where tourists go to darken skin
35 And dealers like to sell guns there
I just can't tell you what's the price.

I am told I have no country now
I am told I am a lie
I am told that modern history books
40 May forget my name.

We can all be refugees
Sometimes it only takes a day,
Sometimes it only takes a handshake
Or a paper that is signed.
45 We all came from refugees
Nobody simply just appeared,
Nobody's here without a struggle,
And why should we live in fear
Of the weather or the troubles?
50 We all came here from somewhere.

Benjamin Zephaniah, "We Refugees", http://benja
minzephaniah.com [31.05.2015]

ZOOM IN: People

Sir Paul Collier, born in Sheffield, UK, in 1949, is Professor of Economics at the University of Oxford and a specialist in the political, economic and developmental predicaments of poor countries. In 2010 and 2011, his name appeared on the *Foreign Policy* magazine list of top global thinkers. In 2014, he was knighted for his services in promoting research and policy change in Africa.

M5 Exodus: Mass Migration as a Response to Global Inequality
Paul Collier

1. Before reading the excerpt from Collier's book, look up a definition of the noun 'exodus' and study the word cloud. Then predict what the text will centre around. In your prediction, employ what you already know about refugee issues (cf. M4).

2. Now read task no. 3 and scan the text for the information required to fulfil this task. Organise your findings in an appropriate graphical form (cf. skills pages).

3. Based on your visualisation, **state** the causes and effects of global exoduses.

4. **Analyse** Collier's line of argument as well as the style, tone and register of his text. Draw a conclusion from your analysis regarding a. Collier's attitude towards international migration and b. his target readers and their social status.

5. "In most societies for most of history high diversity has been a handicap. Even within modern Europe, the relatively modest cultural difference between Germans and Greeks has stretched to breaking the limited institutional harmonization achieved by the European Union." (ll. 31–34). **Comment** on Collier's argument, taking into account the so-called 'Grexit' or 'Graccident' discussion.

ZOOM IN: Terminology

'Grexit' is a portmanteau [pɔːt'mæntəʊ] combining the words 'Greece' and 'exit', referring to the possibility that Greece could leave the Eurozone. So what does 'Graccident' mean?

Mass international migration is a response to extreme global inequality. As never before, young people in the poorest countries are aware of opportunities elsewhere. That inequality opened up over the past two centuries and will close during the coming century. Most developing countries are now rapidly converging* on the high-income countries: this is

5 the great story of our time. Mass migration is therefore not a permanent feature of globalization. Quite the contrary, it is a temporary response to an ugly phase in which prosperity has not yet globalized. A century from now, the world will be far more integrated than now in respect to trade, information, and finance, but the net flow of migration will have diminished*.

10 Although international migration responds to global inequality, it does not significantly change it. What is driving economic convergence* is the transformation of the social models prevailing in poor societies. Gradually, their institutions are becoming more inclusive* and less the preserve* of extractive* elites. Their economic narratives* are shifting from the zero-sum* mentality of grievance* to recognition of the scope* for positive-

15 sum* cooperation. Loyalties are gradually expanding from clans to nations. Organizations are learning how to make workers more productive by combining scale with motivation*. These profound changes are being achieved through adapting global ideas to local contexts. As social models strengthen and economies grow, migration from rural poverty indeed matters, but the journey is to Lagos and Mumbai, not London and Madrid.

20 Yet although international migration is a transient* sideshow to convergence, it may leave permanent legacies*. One sure legacy that is unambiguously benign* is that the high-income societies have become multiracial. Given their past history of racism, the revolution in sentiments consequent upon intermarriage and coexistence has been profoundly liberating for all concerned.

25 But in the absence of effective migration policies, migration will continue to accelerate, and this could imply other possible legacies. The currently high-income countries could become postnational, multicultural societies. On the hopeful new view of multiculturalism propounded* by Western elites, this would also be benign: such societies would be stimulating and prosperous. But the track record* of culturally diverse societies is not so

30 encouraging that this is the only possible outcome from an unlimited increase in diversity. In most societies for most of history high diversity has been a handicap. Even within modern Europe, the relatively modest cultural difference between Germans and Greeks has stretched to breaking the limited institutional harmonization achieved by the European Union. It is possible that permanently rising cultural diversity would gradually un-

35 dermine* mutual regard and that unabsorbed diasporas* would hang onto dysfunctional aspects of the social models that prevailed in their countries of origin at the time of migration. A further possible legacy of a continuing acceleration in migration is that small, poor countries like Haiti that can offer little to their most talented people would suffer an ac-

---

economic convergence *cf. vocabulary box*
to diminish to become less in size
inclusive vs. extractive *cf. vocabulary box*
preserve sanctuary
narrative account
zero-sum (*adj.*) **vs. positive-sum** (*adj.*) *cf. vocabulary box*
grievance a feeling of having been treated unfairly
scope opportunity for unhampered activity
combining scale with motivation Motivation Assessment Scale (MAS), a tool to respond effectively to behaviour

transient not lasting long

legacy inheritance, heritage, something transmitted from the past
benign [bɪ'naɪn] favourable

to propound to suggest (an idea, a theory)
track record a record of past performance often taken as an indicator of likely future performance

to undermine to weaken
diaspora people settled far from their ancestral homelands

h(a)emorrhage ['hɛmərɪdʒ] *here:* a rapid and uncontrollable loss or outflow

celerating hemorrhage* of capabilities: an exodus. They are already beyond the point at
40 which emigration is beneficial. While the fortunate would leave, those left behind might be unable to catch up with the rest of mankind.

Meanwhile, the emerging high-income societies are likely to become less multicultural. As part of the gradual transformation of their social models, identities will have enlarged from the fragmentation of clans to the unifying sense of the nation. In embracing the
45 benign uses of nationalism, they will come to resemble the old high-income countries

prior (to) before

prior* to migration.

Periodically, over the centuries the fortunes of societies have reversed. North America overtook Latin America; Europe overtook China. The financial crisis, with its source and effects in the high-income societies, has dented* the smug complacency* by which their

to dent to have a weakening effect (on) **smug complacency** a feeling of being highly self-satisfied

50 citizens took economic superiority for granted. That most societies will catch up with the West is now accepted. But convergence may not be the end of the story. Singapore, which in 1950 was much poorer than Europe, is now much richer. If social models really are the fundamental determinants of prosperity, the rise of multiculturalism in one part of the world, coincident* with its decline* elsewhere, could have surprising implications.

coincident happening at the same time **decline** the process of becoming worse in condition or quality

Paul Collier, *Exodus: Immigration and Multiculturalism in the 21st Century*, Penguin, London 2013, pp. 271–273

Zoom in: Vocabulary

Commercialese or economic jargon

- **Economic convergence** is the hypothesis that per capita incomes of poorer economies will grow faster than those of richer economies. As a result, all economies should eventually **converge** (i.e. meet at a point) in terms of per capita income.
- In poorer economies, resources are being **extracted** from the many by the few (i.e. **extractive** elites) who, thus, maximise their riches at the expense of the poor. In contrast, **inclusive** economies distribute power more widely, have secure property rights and free-market systems.
- A situation is **zero-sum** if whatever is gained by one side will be lost by the other side, whereas it is **positive-sum** if one party does not benefit at the expense of another party.

---

6. ▷ **Analyse** the given data and **explain** what they reveal about migration flows to Europe (cf. skills & vocabulary box).

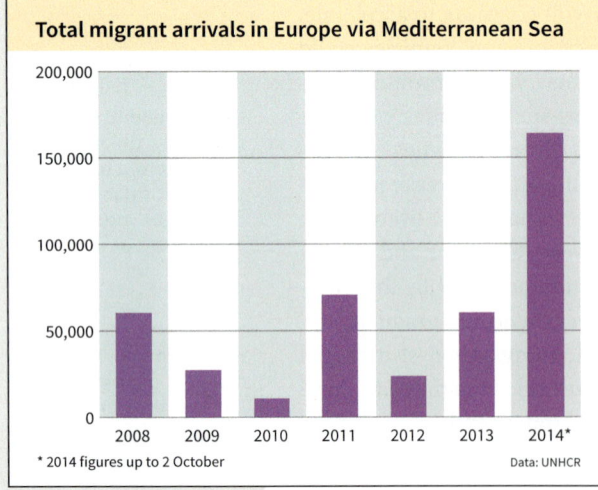

Total migrant arrivals in Europe via Mediterranean Sea
* 2014 figures up to 2 October
Data: UNHCR

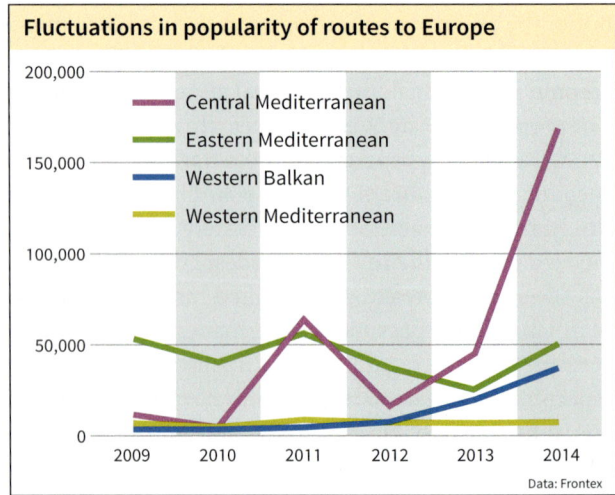

Fluctuations in popularity of routes to Europe
Data: Frontex

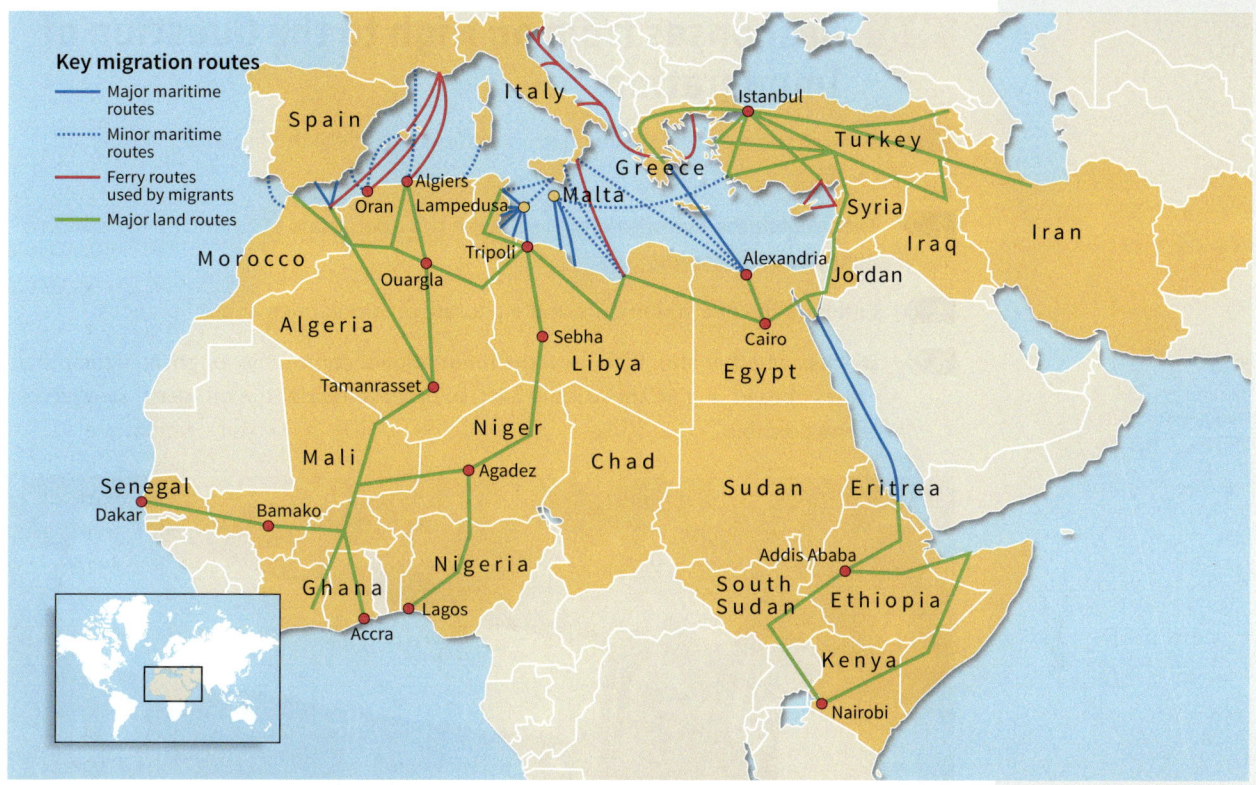

Key migration routes
— Major maritime routes
····· Minor maritime routes
— Ferry routes used by migrants
— Major land routes

ZOOM IN: Skills & Vocabulary

Analysing maps, graphs, diagrams, and tables

Maps, graphs, diagrams, and tables are visual representations used to either organise information so that it is easier to see patterns, trends, and relationships or to show the significant features and findings of an investigation in terms of the relationships between the units of measurement.

Task 6 asks you to analyse (1) a **map** showing trends at a specific point of time, 2) a **line chart** and (3) a (vertical) **bar chart**, both depicting changes over a period of time.

Remember to describe what you can see before drawing conclusions.

Useful words and expressions for talking about visual representations

- *The map/graph shows/depicts/illustrates/outlines/represents ...*
- Basic elements of a **map**: *(bluish/greyish/beige-coloured/shaded ...) areas stand for/represent/are located in/are distributed equally/unequally ...; the (green/red/coloured ...) lines show/visualise/mark/indicate ...;*
- Basic trends of a **map**: *the lines/routes/flows run parallel/converge/intersect/zigzag/span/follow/lead to/across/ beyond ... frontiers/countries/oceans/cities/harbours ...; there is a concentration of ... in the north/south/west/east ...*
- Basic elements of a **graph**: *the vertical/horizontal axis/to reach a peak/a low point/a straight line/a (bumpy) curve ...*
- The four basic trends of a **graph**:
  Upward movement ↗: *to increase/to rise/to grow/to climb/to jump/to skyrocket/to reach a (an all-time) peak ...; an increase/a rise/a boom/a growth/an upswing ...;*
  Downward movement ↘: *to decrease/to fall (off)/to drop/to decline/to collapse/to bottom out ...; a decrease/a cut/a fall/a drop/a downswing/a decline/a collapse (dramatic fall) ...;*
  No movement →: *to remain stable/to stay constant/to stabilise ...; stabilisation ...*
  Change of direction ↘ or ↗: *to level off/out/to stop falling/rising/to remain steady ...; a levelling off/a change ...;*
- Degree of change: *dramatic(ally)/significant(ly)/considerable(bly)/moderate(ly)/slight(ly) ...;*
- Speed of change: *rapid(ly)/swift(ly)/quick(ly)/gradual(ly)/gentle(ly)/little by little/slow(ly) ...*

M6 Responses from on High to the Question of Immigration

1. ⟫ **Sum** up the main message on immigration of each of the five speech excerpts (**A – E**).

2. ⟫ Then match the five speakers (**1 – 5**) with the quotations you find appropriate. **Justify** your decisions.

3. ⟫ **Compare** the five statements and elaborate on similarities and differences.

4. ⟫ **Discuss** whether and, if so, how the international community ought to defend our values abroad, e. g. in the Middle East, in order to render the refugees' safe return home possible.

Since Italy began rescuing Africans from the Mediterranean after the major tragedy in April 2015, the number of refugees coming to Europe has risen dramatically.

particularistic paying exclusive attention to one's own particular interests
to assert to state in a definite way

A "[...] there needs to be a united response to the question of migration. We cannot allow the Mediterranean to become a vast cemetery! The boats landing daily on the shores of Europe are filled with men and women who need acceptance and assistance. The absence of mutual support within the European Union runs the risk of encouraging particularistic* solutions to the problem, solutions which fail to take into account the human dignity ⁵ of immigrants, and thus contribute to slave labour and continuing social tensions. Europe will be able to confront the problems associated with immigration only if it is capable of clearly asserting* its own cultural identity and enacting adequate legislation to protect the rights of European citizens and to ensure the acceptance of immigrants. Only if it is capable of adopting fair, courageous and realistic policies which can assist the countries ¹⁰ of origin in their own social and political development and in their efforts to resolve internal conflicts – the principal cause of this phenomenon – rather than adopting policies motivated by self-interest, which increase and feed such conflicts. We need to take action against the causes and not only the effects."

to boil down to to be simplifiable or summarisable as

B "It is not wrong to express concern about the scale of people coming into the country. ¹⁵ People have understandably become frustrated. It boils down* to one word: control. People want Government to have control over the numbers of people coming here and the

circumstances in which they come, both from around the world and from within the European Union. They want control over who has the right to receive benefits and what is
20 expected of them in return. They want to know that foreign criminals can be excluded – or if already here, removed. And they want us to manage carefully the pressures on our schools, our hospitals and our housing. If we are to maintain this successful open meritocratic* democracy we treasure, we have to maintain faith in government's ability to control the rate at which people come to [this country]. [...] We must have no truck* with
25 those who use immigration to foment* division, or as a surrogate* for other agendas. We should distrust those who sell the snake oil* of simple solutions. There are no simple solutions. Managing immigration is hard. Not only here. But in every major developed economy."

C "[...] our tradition of welcoming immigrants from around the world has given us a tre-
30 mendous advantage over other nations. It's kept us youthful, dynamic, and entrepreneurial*. It has shaped our character as a people with limitless possibilities – people not trapped by our past, but able to remake ourselves as we choose. But today, our immigration system is broken – and everybody knows it. Families who enter our country the right way and play by the rules watch others flout* the rules. Business owners who offer their
35 workers good wages and benefits see the competition exploit undocumented immigrants by paying them far less. [...] We expect people who live in this country to play by the rules. We expect that those who cut the line will not be unfairly rewarded. So we're going to offer the following deal: If you've been in [our country] for more than five years; if you have children who are citizens of [this country] or legal residents; if you register, pass a crimi-
40 nal background check, and you're willing to pay your fair share of taxes – you'll be able to apply to stay in this country temporarily without fear of deportation. You can come out of the shadows and get right with the law."

D "The humanitarian disaster in Syria [...] has cost far too many lives and driven millions of people out of their homes. [Our country] has great respect for the efforts of neighbour-
45 ing countries – Jordan, Lebanon, Turkey, Iraq – which have taken in and are supporting an exceptional number of refugees from Syria. So far around 40,000 refugees have come to [our country]. But this figure is also rising daily. Even though there seems to be little hope of a quick solution to the disaster, the international community will continue unabated* to work towards finding a solution to this crisis. The developments in North Africa
50 and the Middle East show how long and arduous* the way to a stable society can be. [...] On the African continent many states are experiencing remarkable development. A growing middle class is an expression of growing prosperity, which is no longer restricted to a privileged few. However, we are also confronted with persistent* conflicts – allow me to cite the examples of South Sudan and Central Africa at this point. In the long term, peace
55 and stability cannot be created from outside. At the end of the day, the responsibility lies with the regions themselves."

E "Since I was last here in Iraq, another two million people have been forced from their homes. The brutality of the conflict and the speed and scale of the displacement* has shocked the world and help has come but not nearly enough. We are being tested here as
60 an international community and so far, for all the immense efforts and good intentions, the international community is failing. It is past time for leaders on all sides to find a common ground and a way to move forward. It is not enough to defend our values at home, we have to defend them here, in the camps and in the informal settlements across the Middle East, and the ruined towns of Iraq and Syria. Millions of people are internally
65 displaced and over five million people are in dire* need of humanitarian assistance in

---

meritocratic related to a system in which you move ahead on the basis of your achievement
to have no truck with to have no dealings with
to foment to promote the development of something bad
surrogate substitute
snake oil product that is sold as medicine but that is not really beneficial or helpful in any way
entrepreneurial [ˌɒntrəprəˈnɜːrɪəl] enterprising and managing the risks of a business
to flout to break (the rules) without showing shame

unabated continuing at full force
arduous very difficult

persistent continuing without change

displacement the process of forcing (people) to leave the area where they live

dire very urgent

Syria alone. They are paying the price for our collective failure to end the conflict which has allowed extremists to take hold. The people I met today need to know that we will be with them. Giving them the support they need to survive for every day they remain displaced. And above all they need to know that one day they will be able to go home."

1 Angelina Jolie, American actress and activist (25 January 2015)

Solution cf. p. 60

2 Angela Merkel, Federal Chancellor of Germany (11 June 2014)

3 David Cameron, Prime Minister of the UK (20 November 2014)

4 His Holiness Pope Francis (25 November 2014)

5 Barack Obama, 44th President of the USA (20 November 2014)

M7 Living in a Limbo State

M7a Capital

John Lanchester

John Lanchester is a British journalist and novelist. In the excerpt from his novel *Capital*, we meet traffic warden Quentina, who has exchanged political activism in Zimbabwe for encounters with enraged motorists in London.

1. ▷ **Point out** why and how the protagonist took refuge in England and **describe** the obstacles she has had to overcome over there.

2. ▷ **Characterise** the protagonist and **examine** the way she is presented.

3. ▷ Having arrived in England illegally, the protagonist is forced to live in a "limbo state" (l. 13). Against the backdrop of European immigration policy, **assess** Quentina's situation as a political refugee.

John Lanchester (born in Hamburg, Germany, in 1962)

Harare largest city and capital of Zimbabwe, cf. the map on p. 47
goon a person hired to rough someone up, usually someone big and dumb who commits acts of violence for money

Quentina's situation was this. In Harare* in the summer of 2003 she had been arrested, interrogated, beaten, released by the police, snatched by goons* on her way home, taken to a house, told that she had seventy-two hours to leave the country, then beaten and left by the roadside. After being treated in hospital she had been smuggled out of the country by missionaries, and came to England on a student visa which she had always intended to overstay. To make a long story short, she had overstayed on purpose, applied for asylum, been rejected, been arrested and sentenced to deportation, but the judge at the final appeal had ruled that she could not be sent back to Zimbabwe because there were grounds for thinking that if she was she would be killed. At that point Quentina had entered a legal state of semi-existence. She had no right to work and could claim only subsistence-level benefits, but she couldn't be imprisoned and deported. She was not a citizen of the UK but she could not go anywhere else. She was a non-person.

The limbo state* in which she was supposed to live did not correspond with reality: she had no right to do the things she needed to do to stay sane and solvent. Fortunately, Quen-
15 tina's lawyer knew of a charity that took in people like her, the Refuge. This was a group that addressed the needs of stateless people and owned a series of properties around the country. It was in this way that Quentina had come to be living in a terraced house in Toot-ing* with six other stateless women and a house manager. The charity split nationalities up because it didn't like the idea of national cliques developing in the different houses
20 and it thought that refugees learned English more quickly if they weren't with their own language group. That was a mistake in Quentina's view, but it was their charity, not hers, so she shared the house with a Sudanese woman, a Kurd, a Chinese woman who had ar-rived the day before and so far had not spoken, an Algerian, and two Eastern European women whose precise nationalities Quentina did not know.
25 Living in the Refuge house with these people was not straightforward*. Work was even less so. The charity supplied food to its 'clients' – that was the word – but could not, le-gally, pay them. Quentina found she had no ability to do nothing all day and that sitting around the house, and not having any disposable income of her own, gave her acute claustrophobia – a sense of being trapped, powerless, inside her own head. This was
30 made worse by the fact that she was, in actuality, genuinely powerless, with no ability to affect her own destiny in any of the relevant important ways. So she decided that she would have to do something with her days, would have to work, in order not to go insane. There was a kind of grapevine* among the refugees on exactly this issue, and that was how she came to encounter 'Kwame Lyons'. He was known as someone who knew some-
35 one who could get identity papers for you and therefore through whom you could find work, as long as you were willing to pay him his cut. Quentina had no idea for how many people he provided this service, but she knew there was no way she was Lyons's only – that word again – 'client'. She didn't know and didn't want to know
40 how many 'clients' Lyons had, how he got hold of the identity papers, whether he used the identity 'Kwame Lyons' with all his clients, how much money
45 he was making, or his real name.
Quentina had been told that one of the best places to go and work was a minicab company known
50 to hire drivers with dodgy* pa-perwork, but she also heard that a. they didn't employ women and b. the company was owned by one of the big South London
55 crime families, as a way of laun-dering* cash. The fake ID pa-pers were enough illegality for Quentina, who was tempera-mentally law-abiding* and who
60 also thought that staying on the

The Zimbabwean government launched an aggressive land re-form program in 2000, resulting in the shutting down of large farms. The majority of black labourers lost their jobs and their homes. Violent gangs, allegedly composed of military veter-ans, forced them to flee with their families.

limbo state state of uncertainty, an intermedi-ate or transitional state; on hold

Tooting district in South London

straightforward easy to do or understand

grapevine circulation of gossip or rumour from person to person

dodgy doubtful, possibly false or dishonest

to launder to process (something acquired illegally) to make it appear respectable
law-abiding obeying the law

right side of the law was good practical policy. There was a certain irony that her entire existence was lawless and stateless, but never mind. So she acted on advice from a traffic warden she met in the street, a man from Zambia, who told her about Control Services and the fact that they hired a high proportion of West and Southern Africans. She had taken her fake ID, filled out a form, filled out another form as part of a test, and got the 65 job, and here she was eighteen months later, [...] a Control Services employee.

John Lanchester, *Capital*, Faber and Faber, London 2012, pp. 131–133

M7b The Embassy of Cambodia

Zadie Smith

Zadie Smith (born in London, UK, in 1975)

Zadie Smith is an English novelist, essayist, and short story writer, whose novel *White Teeth* was included in *TIME* magazine's *TIME 100 Best English-language Novels from 1923 to 2005* list. Her latest short story, *The Embassy of Cambodia*, is set in Willesden in North West London, where Fatou, the protagonist, is staying as a maid-of-all-work for the Derawals, a well-to-do family of Pakistani descent.

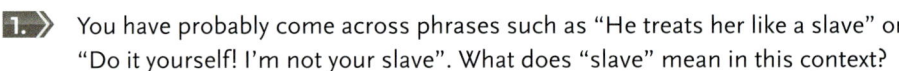

1. You have probably come across phrases such as "He treats her like a slave" or "Do it yourself! I'm not your slave". What does "slave" mean in this context?

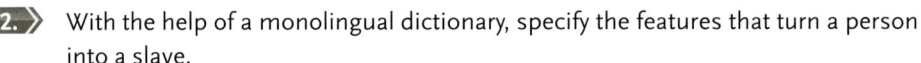

2. With the help of a monolingual dictionary, specify the features that turn a person into a slave.

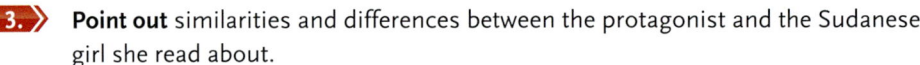

3. **Point out** similarities and differences between the protagonist and the Sudanese girl she read about.

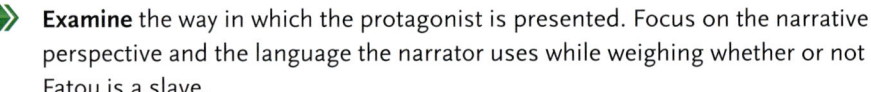

4. **Examine** the way in which the protagonist is presented. Focus on the narrative perspective and the language the narrator uses while weighing whether or not Fatou is a slave.

5. **Comment** on the conclusion Fatou draws in the last line of the excerpt.

to discard to throw away
Metro a free newspaper published in the UK

Accra the capital and largest city of Ghana, cf. map

to retain to keep

In a discarded* Metro* found on the floor of the Derawal kitchen, Fatou read with interest a story about a Sudanese "slave" living in a rich man's house in London. It was not the first time that Fatou had wondered if she herself was a slave, but this story, brief as it was, confirmed in her own mind that she was not. After all, it was her father, and not a kidnapper, who had taken her from Ivory Coast to Ghana, and when they reached Accra* they 5 had both found employment in the same hotel. Two years later, when she was eighteen, it was her father again who had organized her difficult passage to Libya and then on to Italy – a not insignificant financial sacrifice on his part. Also, Fatou could read English – and speak a little Italian – and this girl in the paper could not read or speak anything except the language of her tribe. And nobody beat Fatou, although Mrs Derawal had twice 10 slapped her in the face, and the two older children spoke to her with no respect at all and thanked her for nothing. (Sometimes she heard her name used as a term of abuse between them. "You're as black as Fatou." Or "You're as stupid as Fatou.") On the other hand, just like the girl in the newspaper, she had not seen her passport with her own eyes since she arrived at the Derawals', and she had been told from the start that her wages 15 were to be retained* by the Derawals to pay for the food and water and heat she would require during her stay, as well as to cover the rent for the room she slept in. In the final

analysis, however, Fatou was not confined* to the house. She had an Oyster Card*, given to her by the Derawals, and was trusted to do the food shopping and other outside tasks,
20 for which she was given cash and told to return with change and receipts for everything. If she did not go out in the evenings that was only because she had no money with which to go out, and anyway knew very few people in London. Whereas the girl in the paper was not allowed to leave her employers' premises*, not ever – she was a prisoner.

On Sunday mornings, for example, Fatou regularly left the house, to meet her church
25 friend Andrew Okonkwo at the 98 bus stop and go with him to worship* at the Sacred Heart of Jesus, just off the Kilburn High Road. Afterwards Andrew always took her to a Tunisian café, where they had coffee and cake, which Andrew, who worked as a night guard in the City, always paid for. And on Mondays Fatou swam. In very warm water, and thankful for the semi-darkness in which the health club, for some reason, kept its clien-
30 tele, as if the place were a nightclub, or a midnight Mass. The darkness helped disguise the fact that her swimming costume was in fact a sturdy* black bra and a pair of plain black cotton knickers. No, on balance she did not think she was a slave.

Zadie Smith, *The Embassy of Cambodia*, Köln: Kiepenheuer & Witsch, 2014, pp. 78–80

to confine to keep someone in a place that they cannot leave
Oyster Card a form of electronic ticketing used on public transport in Greater London
premises the buildings and land that someone uses or owns
to worship to pray to a god in a religious building

sturdy solid, durable

The majority of Ivorian refugees fled Ivory Coast during the post-electoral violence in 2010/2011. The crisis began when the opposition candidate launched a military offensive, backed by French forces, which ended with the capture of the President.

6. **Compare** the situation of Quentina and Fatou. Use a table or the Venn diagram (cf. skills pages) to illustrate similarities and differences.

Malala (born in Mingora, Pakistan, in 1997)

M8 Education for Girls

Malala Yousafzai

When the Taliban took control of Pakistan's Swat Valley, one girl spoke out. Malala Yousafzai refused to be silenced and fought for her right to an education. On Tuesday, 9 October 2012, she was shot in the head while riding the bus home from school. At sixteen, Malala has become a global symbol of peaceful protest and the youngest person ever to receive the Nobel Peace Prize.

1. Tell the story of the Taliban's assassination attempt on Malala, as shown in the comic.

2. Research Malala's fund (www.malala.org), launched to empower girls through education. Note key words concerning the fund's initiatives, copy them onto an overhead transparency and give a short talk in class, speaking freely with the aid of your key words only.

3. **Outline** why Malala rejected the Taliban commander's offer to return to Pakistan and the view she advances of the Taliban in general.

4. **Characterise** Malala and **explain** why she is an inspiration to girls around the globe.

5. Put yourself in the shoes of one of the girls from the slums in Nairobi, Kenya, attending *NairoBits*, an informal education program with a focus on information and communications technology. Prepare to contact Malala via her homepage, thanking her for being given the opportunity to attend secondary school and learn tech-skills free of charge.

(panel #1)

(panel #2)

(panel #3)

(panel #4)

(panel #5)

(panel #6)

(panel #7)

to malign [mə'laɪn] to say bad things about (someone or something) publicly
madrasa a Muslim school, college, or university that is often part of a mosque
Mohammed Hanif a Pakistani writer and journalist

Jani (mun) Persian term of endearment meaning 'soul mate'

illiterate not knowing how to write or read

Karachi *cf. map*
to toss to throw with a quick, light motion

to hurl to throw with force
Quetta *cf. map*

Gilgit(-Baltistan) formerly known as Northern Areas, *cf. map*

The most surprising letter I got after my speech was from a Taliban commander who recently escaped from prison. His name was Adnan Rashid and he used to be in the Pakistan air force. He had been in jail since 2003 for attempting to assassinate President Musharraf. He said the Taliban had attacked me not for my campaign for education but because I tried to 'malign* [their] efforts to establish the Islamic system'. He said he was writing to me because he was shocked by my shooting and wished he could have warned me beforehand. He wrote that they would forgive me if I came back to Pakistan, wore a burqa and went to a madrasa*.

Journalists urged me to answer him, but I thought, *Who is this man to say that?* The Taliban are not our rulers. It's my life, how I live it is my choice. But Mohammed Hanif* wrote an article pointing out that the good thing about the Taliban letter was that many people claim I wasn't shot, yet here they were accepting responsibility.

I know I will go back to Pakistan, but whenever I tell my father I want to go home, he finds excuses. 'No, *Jani**, your treatment is not complete', he says, or, 'These schools are good. You should stay here and gather knowledge so you can use your words powerfully.'

He is right. I want to learn and be trained well with the weapon of knowledge. Then I will be able to fight more effectively for my cause.

Today we all know education is our basic right. Not just in the West; Islam too has given us this right. Islam says every girl and every boy should go to school. In the Quran it is written, God wants us to have knowledge. He wants us to know why the sky is blue and about oceans and stars. I know it's a big struggle – around the world there are fifty-seven million children who are not in primary school, thirty-two million of them girls. Sadly my own country Pakistan is one of the worst places: 5.1 million children don't even go to primary school even though in our constitution it says every child has that right. We have almost fifty million illiterate* adults, two-thirds of whom are women, like my own mother.

Girls continue to be killed and schools blown up. In March there was an attack on a girls' school in Karachi* that we had visited. A bomb and a grenade were tossed* into the school playground just as a prize-giving ceremony was about to start. The headmaster, Abdur Rasheed, was killed and eight children hurt between the ages of five and ten. One eight-year-old was left disabled. When my mother heard the news, she cried and cried. 'When our children are sleeping we wouldn't even disturb a hair on their heads', she said, 'but there are people who have guns and shoot them or hurl* bombs. They don't care that their victims are children.' The most shocking attack was in June in the city of Quetta* when a suicide bomber blew up a bus taking forty pupils to their all-girls' college. Fourteen of them were killed. The wounded were followed to the hospital and some nurses were shot.

It's not just the Taliban killing children. Sometimes it's drone attacks, sometimes it's wars, sometimes it's hunger. And sometimes it's their own family. In June two girls my age were murdered in Gilgit*, which is a little north of Swat, for posting a video online showing themselves dancing in the rain wearing traditional dress and headscarves. Apparently their own stepbrother shot them.

Today Swat is more peaceful than other places, but there are still military everywhere, four

years after they supposedly*
removed the Taliban. [...]
Our valley, which was once a
haven for tourists, is now
55 seen as a place of fear. For-
eigners who want to visit
have to get a No Objection
Certificate* from the au-
thorities in Islamabad*. Ho-
60 tels and craft shops are empty. It will be a long time
before tourists return.

Malala Yousafzai, *I Am Malala*, Wei-
denfeld & Nicolson, London 2013,
pp. 262–264

supposedly allegedly

No Objection Certificate
a document to keep
tracks of visitors
Islamabad *cf. map*

M 9 #BringBackOurGirls – Seven Shocking Facts about *Boko Haram*

1. Watch a video message from the leader of the Islamist militant group *Boko Haram*
in which he claims responsibility for the abduction of nearly 300 schoolgirls in
northeast Nigeria (see Webcode). You will need to read the subtitles to be able to
understand his mixture of Hausa and English. Afterwards, share your impressions
of the video with your classmates.

2. **Summarise** the information the text gives about *Boko Haram*.

3. **Examine** what purpose the article on www.news.com.au serves. Focus on its
structure, the presentation of facts and the general attitude towards the subject.

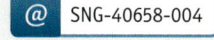 SNG-40658-004

As outrage grows about the kidnapping of nearly 300 Nigerian schoolgirls, it is the first
time that many people are hearing of the extremist group *Boko Haram*. But the organisation has a long history of terrorising people, here are some shocking facts about them:
1. "Western education is a sin"
5 This translation of *Boko Haram's* name has been criticised for not being entirely accurate
but is a rough interpretation. A strict reading of the name suggests that opposition is not
necessarily a blanket* hatred of western education but is targeted specifically at this type
of education being taught in Nigeria. However, kidnapping and threatening to sell off
young girls as slaves seems to indicate that opposition is more than just a protest about
10 the "foreign" school around the corner.
In a video that claimed responsibility for the kidnapping, a representative of the group
flanked by militants holding AK-47s*, says, "I said western education should end." He
then said he planned to sell the girls. "Allah has instructed me to sell them. They are his
property and I will carry out his instructions." [...]
15 **2. It's not just western education that is forbidden**
Boko Haram wants to create a "pure" Islamic state ruled by sharia law*. It reportedly be-
lieves that Muslims should not participate in political or social activities associated with
Western society. This can include voting in elections, wearing shirts and trousers, or re-
ceiving a secular* education.

blanket (*adj.*) general

AK-47 a popular assault
rifle

Sharia [ʃəˈriːə] **law** the
legal framework within
which all aspects of life
are regulated for those
living in a legal system
based on Islam
secular not relating to
religion

to abduct to kidnap

to hawk to offer (goods) for sale

inauguration formal induction into office

3. They kidnap and rape women

Long before they grabbed international headlines for abducting* the teenage girls, they were known for kidnapping women in the street or from farms. "Now they are picking up women anywhere and using them to satisfy themselves", a commander with the anti-*Boko Haram* group, the *Civilian Joint Task Force,* told *Human Rights Watch* in 2013. "Some of the girls we found hiding when we invaded *Boko Haram* camps around Sambisa [Forest] told us they were dragged into vehicles when hawking* on the street. "When we return them home, their families are too ashamed to keep them because nobody will marry a girl who has been raped or has a child from these bad people." 20 25

4. They think it's OK to enslave women

"Girls, you should go and get married," *Boko Haram* leader Abubakar Shekau said in a video. "There is a market for selling humans. Allah says I should sell. He commands me to sell. I will sell women. I sell women." Some women have reportedly been sold into marriage with the militants for as little as $12. Almost half the girls in Nigeria marry before they reach 18 years of age, according to figures from the *United Nations Girls Education Initiative.* Many struggle to get an education, only 66 per cent aged between 15 and 24 years old can read and write. 30 35

5. They believe in violence

Boko Haram has been carrying out terrorist attacks for years and the *International Crisis Group* estimates that the group has killed more than 4000 people in Nigeria in four years. [...] The group is known for using gunmen on motorbikes to kill police, politicians and anyone else who does not support the group, and [...] has been involved in bombings on Christmas Day in 2011, a New Year's Eve attack in 2010, attacks during the inauguration* of President Goodluck Jonathan in 2011 and further bombings on the UN headquarters in Abuja. 40

6. They use child soldiers

Human Rights Watch states that they have recruited children as soldiers including those as young as 12 years old. 45

7. They hate Christians

In a *YouTube* video the group's leader Abubakar Shekau said their targeting of Christians was revenge for previous attacks on Muslims. "Either you are with us, I mean, we are Muslims who are following solid footsteps, or you're with Obama, Francois Hollande, George Bush ... Ban Ki-moon and his people generally, any unbeliever ... kill, kill, kill," Shekau says. "This war is against Christians, I mean Christians generally." [...] 50

"Seven shocking facts about Boko Haram, the group that kidnaps schoolgirls", www.news.com.au, 07.05.2014 [30.05.2015]

ZOOM IN: Organisations

- The *Civilian Joint Task Force* is a loose group of militants, formed in Maiduguri, Nigeria, to oust (to force out) *Boko Haram* from their city.
- *Human Rights Watch* is an international non-governmental organisation, conducting research and advocacy on human rights. Its headquarters are in New York City.
- The *United Nations Girls Education Initiative* is an initiative launched by the United Nations in 2000. It aims to give girls equal access to all levels of education. Its headquarters are in Washington, D.C.
- The *International Crisis Group* is a conflict-prevention non-profit organisation that advances policies to prevent, mitigate (to make less severe or intense) or resolve conflict. Its headquarters are in Brussels, Belgium.
- The hashtag *#BringBackOurGirls* was created in the hope of keeping the story in the news. First lady Michelle Obama used it to raise awareness for the girls kidnapped by *Boko Haram* in April 2014.

M 10   ISIS's Teenage Austrian Poster Girl Jihadi Brides

Adam Withnall

1. ⟫ **Outline** the fate of the two Austrian teenagers.

2. ⟫ **Explain** why, according to the Austrian interior ministry, it is scarcely possible to bring back the girls.

3. ⟫ Put yourself in the shoes of either Sabina or Samra. Write an entry in your diary that you have been able to hide from your husband. Focus on the reasons for your wish to return home.

ISIS's teenage Austrian poster girl jihadi* brides "have changed their minds and want to come home". The teenagers have been in contact with their families, officials say.

Two teenage girls who left Austria to travel to Syria and become "jihadi brides" have reportedly grown disillusioned by life with ISIS and told their families they want to return
5 home.

When they first arrived in the Middle East via Turkey, 15-year-old Sabina Selimovic and 17-year-old Samra Kesinovic were used as poster girls for the militant group, and social media posts purported* to show how much fun they were having.

Interpol* became involved when the girls left Austria in April, despite the fact that they
10 wrote a note telling their parents: "Don't look for us. We will serve Allah – and we will die for him."

But now the Austrian government has said the girls want to come back, and have been in contact with their families, the Austrian newspaper *Österreich* reported.

Speaking to the paper, an official with the home office said that escaping ISIS in Syria
15 "after such a long time" would be extremely difficult.

Austrian media reports suggest that the girls have been married to Chechen* fighters and that they may be pregnant – and even if they could flee, Austria's laws bar* them from returning once they have joined a foreign war.

Karl-Heinz Grunboeck, a spokesperson for the Austrian interior ministry, said: "The
20 main problem is about people coming back to Austria. Once they leave, this is almost impossible."

jihadi [dʒɪˈhædi] an Islamic fundamentalist who participates in **jihad**, a war fought by Muslims to defend or spread their beliefs

to purport to claim, esp. falsely
Interpol International Criminal Police Organisation

Chechen [tʃəˈtʃɛn] member of the predominant, traditionally Muslim ethnic group of Chechnya [ˈtʃɛtʃnyɒ]
to bar to officially forbid, prohibit, prevent

Sabina Selimovic, 15, (left) and Samra Kesinovic, 17, in pictures posted to social media profiles apparently from within Syria (Interpol)

to commandeer to seize for public or military use
to doctor to alter or modify for a specific end

Levant [lɪˈvænt] a former name for the area, now occupied by Lebanon, Syria, and Israel
affiliates *here:* groups associated with *ISIL/ISIS* as subordinate members
caliphate [ˈkælə,feɪt] the office, jurisdiction, or reign of a caliph
defunct no longer valid
ethnic cleansing [ˈklenzɪŋ] the expulsion, imprisonment, or killing of an ethnic minority by a dominant majority in order to achieve ethnic homogeneity
to resurrect to cause (something that had ended) to exist again

Experts now believe that the social media accounts associated to the girls were commandeered* by ISIS, with images and posts doctored* to encourage other girls to follow suit. An unnamed security service source told the *Austrian Times*: "It is clear that whoever is
25   operating their pages it probably is not the girls, and that they are being used for propaganda."
Sabina and Samra grew up in Vienna in Bosnian immigrant families, according to the Austrian media, but their views are believed to have become increasingly radical in recent years. In total, around 130 Austrian nationals are believed to have become foreign fighters
30   for ISIS.

Adam Withnall, "ISIS's Teenage Austrian Poster Girl Jihadi Brides 'have changed their minds and want to come home'", www.independent.co.uk, 12.10.2014 [31.03.2015]

ZOOM IN: Terminology

ISIL [ˈaɪsəl] (*Islamic State of Iraq and the Levant**) or **ISIS** [ˈaɪsɪs] (*Islamic State of Iraq and Syria*) is an Islamic extremist rebel group ruling by Sharia law and controlling territory in Syria, Iraq, and Libya, with operations or affiliates* in Lebanon, Nigeria, Egypt, and other areas of the Middle East, North Africa, West Africa, South Asia, and Southeast Asia. The group's goal is to establish a caliphate* in Iraq and al-Sham, whose broadest geographic definition is close to the now-defunct* term "Levant." The United Nations has held ISIL/ISIS responsible for human rights abuses and war crimes; Amnesty International has reported ethnic cleansing* by the group on a "historic scale".

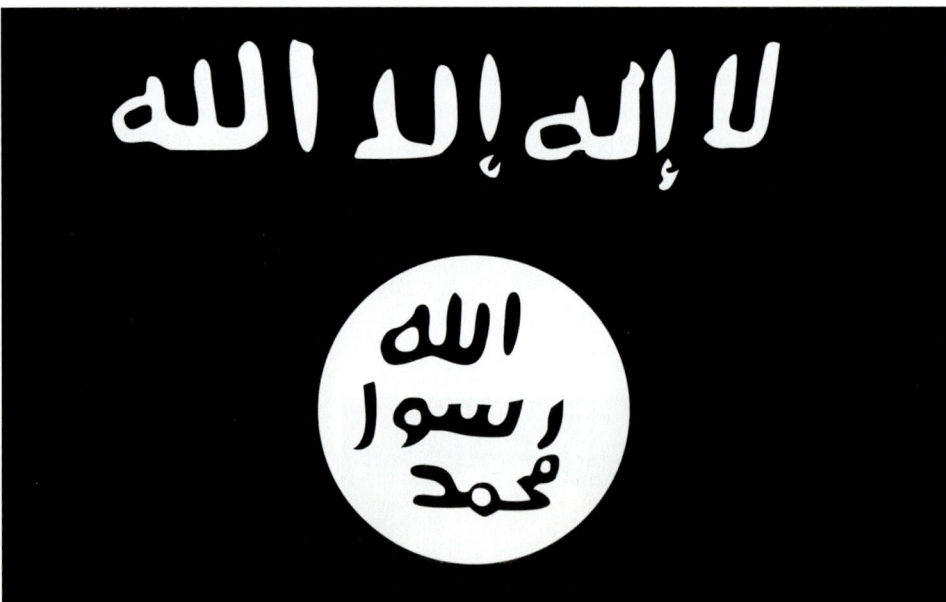

According to Jonathan Bloom, Professor of Islamic Art at Boston College, the black-and-white *ISIL/ISIS* flag relates to the 8th century when the Second Dynasty of Islam came to power with black banners. The white writing at the top of the flag is the first half of an Islamic phrase called the *shahada*, or declaration of faith, which reads: "There is no god but God." The white circle at its centre contains the second part of the *shahada*: "Muhammad is the Messenger of God." The two Arabic phrases, the black colour of the flag and the ancient-looking Arabic font evoke an image of the historical Islamic caliphate that *ISIL/ISIS* claims to have resurrected*.

Nina Porzucki, "Ever wonder what this black-and-white flag means?", www.pri.org, 04.09.2014 [30.05.2015]

to resurrect to cause (something that had ended) to exist again

M 11 Islamist Terror Attacks

1. ▶ **Point out** why Islamist terrorism affects non-Westerners to a greater extent than Westerners.

2. ▶ **Analyse** the data given in the two charts below (cf. M 5, skills & vocabulary box) and **explain** what they reveal about Islamist terror in Western Europe and worldwide.

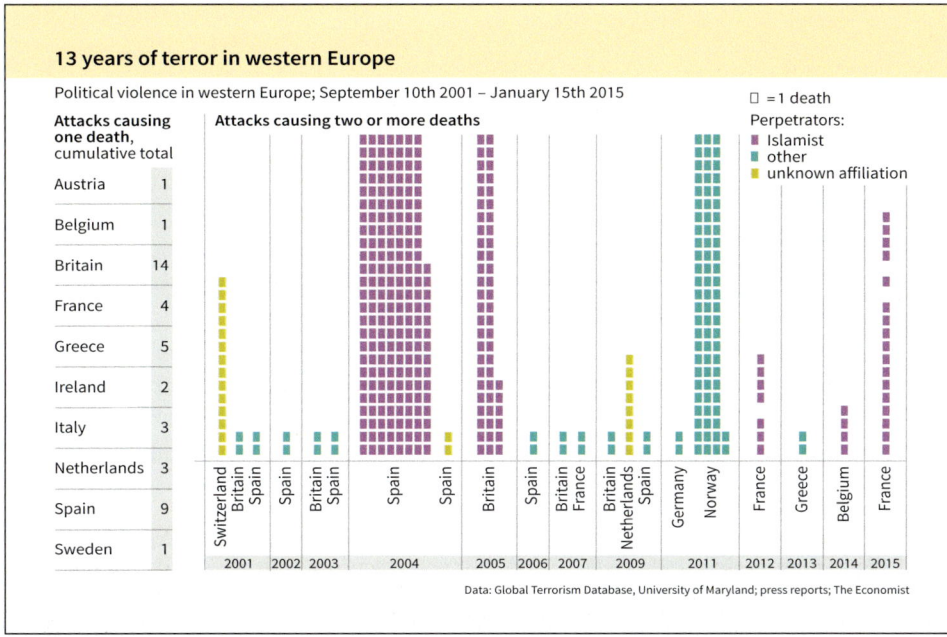

13 years of terror in western Europe

Political violence in western Europe; September 10th 2001 – January 15th 2015

□ = 1 death
Perpetrators:
■ Islamist
■ other
■ unknown affiliation

Attacks causing one death, cumulative total

Austria	1
Belgium	1
Britain	14
France	4
Greece	5
Ireland	2
Italy	3
Netherlands	3
Spain	9
Sweden	1

Data: Global Terrorism Database, University of Maryland; press reports; The Economist

Europe has suffered many Islamist terrorist attacks in recent years, but before the assault* on Charlie Hebdo, only two of them caused more than ten deaths: the Madrid train attack in May 2004 and the London tube and bus bombings 14 months later. Various factors threaten to mar* this broadly reassuring picture. The civil wars in Libya, Yemen and

A month of terror worldwide

Selected terrorist attacks by Islamist groups

Legend: Europe | Africa | Middle East | Asia/Oceania

Date	Location	Group considered responsible*	Primary method	Number of dead
December 2014				
15th	Sydney, Australia	Unknown affiliation	Gun attack	2
16th	Peschawar, Pakistan	Taliban	Gun attack	148
16th	Rada'a district, Yemen	Unknown affiliation	Suicide bombing	25
18th	Gumsuri, Nigeria	Boko Haram	Gun attack	32
22nd	Gombe, Nigeria	Boko Haram	Bombing	20
24th	Madaen, Iraq	Unknown affiliation	Suicide bombing	33
25th	Mogadishu, Somalia	Shabab	Gun attack	9
26th	Mozogo district, Cameroon	Boko Haram	Unknown	23
January 2015				
3rd	Baga, Nigeria	Boko Haram	Gun attack	150
7th	Sana'a, Yemen	Unknown affiliation	Suicide bombing	37
7th	Paris, France	Unknown affiliation	Gun attack	12
8th	Paris, France	Unknown affiliation	Gun attack	1
9th	Paris, France	Unknown affiliation	Gun attack	4
10th	Maiduguri, Nigeria	Boko Haram	Suicide bombing	19
10th	Tripoli, Lebanon	Nusra Front	Suicide bombing	7
11th	Potiskum, Nigeria	Boko Haram	Suicide bombing	4
13th	Gombe, Nigeria	Unknown affiliation	Suicide bombing	2

* Including claims of responsibility

Data: Press reports; The Economist

cumulative [ˈkjuːmjulətiv] becoming greater by additions
perpetrator someone who has committed a crime
affiliation a connection with (an organisation)

assault a violent physical attack

to mar to spoil

Oceania [əʊʃiˈɑːniə] the region of the world that consists of the islands of the Pacific Ocean and the seas around them

remotely in the slightest
sophistication complexity, as in organisation
life and limb used when talking about situations in which someone could die or be injured
atrocity [əˈtrosəti] behaviour or action that is cruel or ruthless

Syria mean there is a much broader range of places and groups from which threats can 5 come. There has never previously been anything remotely* on the same scale as Islamic State in terms of financial resources, territory and sophistication*. Yet the threat to life and limb* from Islamic terrorism remains far greater for non-Westerners. Within the past month alone, Islamist attacks in Nigeria and in Pakistan, among others, have claimed many more lives than the atrocities* in France. 10

The Data Team, "Terror attacks", www.economist.com, 15.01.2015 [26.03.2015]

M12 The Blame for the *Charlie Hebdo* Murders

George Packer

George Packer (born in Santa Clara, California, U.S., in 1960) is an American journalist, novelist, and playwright, who is best known for his writings for *The New Yorker*, a magazine of reportage, essays, fiction, cartoons, and poetry.

1. In groups of four, research what happened a) in places such as Newtown, Oslo or Peshawar and b) to people like Salman Rushdie and his translators and publisher or Theo van Gogh, as mentioned in the article. Prepare to present your findings in class.

2. **Describe** the terrorist attack on the French satirical weekly *Charlie Hebdo* in Paris on 7 January 2015.

3. **Outline** why Packer calls this attack "only the latest blows delivered by an ideology that has sought to achieve power through terror for decades" (ll. 8/9).

4. **Analyse** Packer's line of argument as well as his use of language and stylistic devices.

5. **Comment** on the significance of the slogan "Je suis Charlie" that spread rapidly via web and e-mail right after the massacre.

to assimilate to bring into conformity with the customs, attitudes, etc., of a nation
nihilistic anarchic, and destructive
atomized split into many groups, factions, etc.
hollow insincere and false

The murders today in Paris are not a result of France's failure to assimilate* two generations of Muslim immigrants from its former colonies. They're not about French military action against the Islamic State in the Middle East, or the American invasion of Iraq before that. They're not part of some general wave of nihilistic* violence in the economically depressed, socially atomized*, morally hollow* West – the Paris version of Newtown 5 or Oslo. Least of all should they be "understood" as reactions to disrespect for religion on the part of irresponsible cartoonists.

They are only the latest blows delivered by an ideology that has sought to achieve power through terror for decades. It's the same ideology that sent Salman Rushdie into hiding for a decade under a death sentence for writing a novel, then killed his Japanese translator 10 and tried to kill his Italian translator and Norwegian publisher. The ideology that murdered three thousand people in the U.S. on September 11, 2001. The one that butchered* Theo van Gogh in the streets of Amsterdam, in 2004, for making a film. The one that has brought mass rape and slaughter to the cities and deserts of Syria and Iraq. That massacred a hundred and thirty-two children and thirteen adults in a school in Peshawar last 15 month. That regularly kills so many Nigerians, especially young ones, that hardly anyone pays attention.

to butcher [ˈbutʃə] to kill brutally

Because the ideology is the product of a major world religion, a lot of painstaking pretzel logic* goes into trying to explain what the violence does, or doesn't, have to do with Islam.

20 Some well-meaning people tiptoe around the Islamic connection, claiming that the carnage* has nothing to do with faith, or that Islam is a religion of peace, or that, at most, the violence represents a "distortion*" of a great religion. (After suicide bombings in Baghdad, I grew used to hearing Iraqis say, "No Muslim would do this.") Others want to lay the blame entirely on the theological content of Islam, as if other religions are more inher-

25 ently* peaceful – a notion belied* by history as well as scripture.

A religion is not just a set of texts but the living beliefs and practices of its adherents*. Islam today includes a substantial minority of believers who countenance*, if they don't actually carry out, a degree of violence in the application of their convictions that is currently unique. *Charlie Hebdo* had been nondenominational* in its satire, sticking its fin-

30 ger into the sensitivities of Jews and Christians, too – but only Muslims responded with threats and acts of terrorism. For some believers, the violence serves a will to absolute power in the name of God, which is a form of totalitarianism called Islamism – politics as religion, religion as politics. "*Allahu Akbar**!" the killers shouted in the street outside *Charlie Hebdo*. They, at any rate, know what they're about.

35 These thoughts don't offer a guide to mitigating* the astonishing surge* in Islamist killing around the world. Rage and condemnation don't do the job, nor is it helpful to alienate* the millions of Muslims who dislike what's being done in the name of their religion. Many of them immediately condemned the attack on *Charlie Hebdo*, in tones of anguish particular to those whose deepest beliefs have been tainted*. The answer always has to be

40 careful, thoughtful, and tailored* to particular circumstances. In France, it will need to include a renewed debate about how the republic can prevent more of its young Muslim citizens from giving up their minds to a murderous ideology – how more of them might come to consider Mustapha Ourrad, a *Charlie Hebdo* copy editor of Algerian descent who was among the victims, a hero. In other places, the responses have to be different, with

45 higher levels of counter-violence.

But the murders in Paris were so specific and so brazen* as to make their meaning quite clear. The cartoonists died for an idea. The killers are soldiers in a war against freedom of thought and speech, against tolerance, pluralism, and the right to offend – against everything decent in a democratic society. So we must all try to be *Charlie*, not just today but

50 every day.

George Packer, "The Blame for the *Charlie Hebdo* Murders", www.newyorker.com, 07.01.2015 [30.05.2015]
© George Packer/*The New Yorker*

pretzel logic fallible, twisted or circular reasoning that when dissected is wrong, does not make sense or does not explain the situation rationally
carnage large-scale killing
distortion a change in perception so that it does not correspond to reality
inherently intrinsically
to belie to show to be false
adherent supporter (of a cause)
to countenance to tolerate and approve
nondenominational not related to any particular religious congregation
Allahu Akbar! [ælǝhu 'akbaː] (*Arabic*) God is most great!
to mitigate to make less severe
surge sudden increase
to alienate to isolate or dissociate emotionally
to taint to become associated with something undesirable, to turn bad
to tailor to adapt for a particular purpose

brazen shameless

JE SUIS CHARLIE

A tribute at the Place de la République in Paris to those killed during the attack on the office of *Charlie Hebdo*

M 13 What and Where Is Global Power?

On 24 September 2014, Abdullah II ibn al-Hussein, King of the Hashemite Kingdom of Jordan since 1999, gave a much acclaimed speech before the 69th United Nations General Assembly, addressing the role of the UN in times of growing threats to global peace and security.

1. Before listening to King Abdullah's speech, make an educated guess as to what threats he is going to focus on. In doing so, take into account what you have learned about global threats in this chapter.

Listening

2. After listening, try to answer the king's initial rhetorical question as to what and where global power is.

SNG-40658-005

3. Research 'Resolution 2178' condemning violent extremism, which was unanimously adopted by the Security Council on 24 September 2014 (see Webcode). Be prepared to present the central operative phrases of the resolution.

4. In groups of four, prepare questions you would like to ask the UN Security Council, expressing your doubts about the binding and assertive character of their resolutions. Put King Abdullah on the Hot Seat and conduct the interview. Remember to include in your questionnaire the unsolved global threats mentioned in this chapter.

ZOOM IN: Terminology

The UN Security Council

Fifteen members: five permanent members with veto power and ten non-permanent members elected by the General Assembly for a two-year term.

Meetings: at any given time when the need arises.

Rotating presidency: Members take turn at holding the presidency of the Security Council for one month.

Primary responsibility: the maintenance of international peace and security.

For more information cf. www.un.org/en/sc/

M 6 – Solutions and acknowledgements:

A 4 – B 3 – C 5 – D 2 – E 1

A: Pope Francis, "Address to the European Parliament", www.vatican.va, 25.11.2014 [30.05.2015]

B: David Cameron, "Speech on Immigration", http://press.conservatives.com, 28.11.2014 [30.05.2015]

C: Barack Obama, "Remarks by the President in Address to the Nation on Immigration", www.whitehouse. gov, 20.11.2014 [30.05.2015]

D: Angela Merkel, "Speech by Federal Chancellor Angela Merkel at the Reception for the Diplomatic Corps at the Federal Chancellery", www.bundesregierung.de, 11.06.2014 [30.05.2015]

E: UN News Centre, "UN refugees envoy Angelina Jolie says international community 'failing' Iraq's displaced", www.un.org, 25.01.2015 [30.05.2015]

Mapping and Modifying Life: Multiple Risks for Our Planet and Us

M1 Our Planet Seen from Outer Space

Interview with Alexander Gerst

Dr Alexander Gerst is a European Space Agency (ESA) astronaut and geophysicist, who was a crew member of the International Space Station from May to November 2014. In this excerpt from an interview with the *Kölner Stadt-Anzeiger*, Gerst, who is called 'Astro Alex' because of his *Twitter* handle, tells us how small and fragile our planet, the "pale blue dot" as he calls it, seems to be when seen from outer space.

1. Watch the earth roll by from the perspective of 'Astro Alex' in a six-minute time-lapse video from outer space (see Webcode). Talk about the video with a partner, exchanging insights and impressions.

2. **Point out** how Gerst's view of the earth has changed during his six months on the ISS for ESA's 'Blue Dot' mission. Your audience will be a group of exchange students from Finland, who speak only broken German but learn English as a second language, so mediate in English (cf. M 9a, p. 26). In your geography course, they told the class that, due to the melting of glaciers, the sea level in the Gulf of Finland is going to rise at an alarming pace. Hence, you can assume that they will be interested in the German astronaut's views on climate protection.

3. Also **explain** to the Finnish students what Gerst means by saying that his overall way of looking at things is humanistic and not political or ethical.

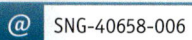
SNG-40658-006

Haben Sie nach einem halben Jahr im Orbit nun einen anderen Blick auf die Erde?
Die Sichtweise auf die Erde hat sich definitiv verändert. Das ist so, wie wenn Sie nach vielen Jahren Ihren früheren Kindergarten besuchen. Da denkt man: Früher kam mir alles so unendlich riesig vor, aber jetzt, fühlt dieser Ort sich so klein an. Ich habe reali-
5 siert, dass unser Planet wirklich klein ist.

@Astro_Alex:
At night, Earth's atmosphere looks most fragile. A thin band of almost nothing, and yet our source of life.
http://twitter.com, 25.06.2014 [31.05.15]

Alexander Gerst (born in Künzelsau, Germany, in 1976)

zerbrechlich fragile	

Und zerbrechlich*?

Man fliegt innerhalb von wenigen Minuten über Kontinente hinweg. Man sieht Hunderte Brände in Afrika, und dass der Amazonas abgeholzt* wird. Von oben sieht man, dass Asche und Luftverschmutzungen* weit in die Atmosphäre getragen werden. Wir gehen nicht sehr achtsam* mit unserer Heimat um. Es gibt nur diesen einen kleinen Planeten 10 im All, auf dem wir Menschen leben können.

Sie sind im All politischer geworden?

Ich sehe das nicht als politisch an. Das ist mehr eine humanistische Sichtweise. Die Erde kennt keine Grenzen. Die Erde interessiert es nicht, ob wir auf ihr leben. Selbst wenn wir Menschen unsere Umwelt zerstören – die Erde wird diese Zerstörung größtenteils* ab- 15 schütteln*. Nur uns wird es dann nicht mehr geben.

Sie könnten als Symbolfigur* für den Klimaschutz werben ...

Ich möchte nicht als Moralapostel* auftreten. Das ist nicht meine Aufgabe. Ich bin Wissenschaftler und Mensch, der zusätzliche Perspektiven vermittelt*. Ich würde mir wünschen, dass jeder Mensch einmal die Erde mit seinen eigenen Augen von oben sehen 20 könnte. Ich bin mir sicher, das verändert unseren Umgang* mit den Dingen. Das sollte sich jeder Teilnehmer einer Klimaschutzkonferenz mal ansehen. Man sieht, wie der Sand von der Sahara über den Atlantik driftet*. Das ist eine riesige Wolke in Gelb und Orange. Die geht bis Brasilien rüber. Da wird einem klar, dass wir beim Klimaschutz weltweit Verantwortung tragen*. 25

Sie haben von oben gesehen, wie der Mensch die Umwelt zerstört. Macht Sie das zum Pessimisten?

Ich bin generell kein Pessimist. Der Mensch ist geboren, um Probleme zu lösen. Wir versuchen das ja mit der Raumfahrt*. Die ESA hat viele Umweltbeobachtungssatelliten*, wir messen* zum Beispiel sogar die Höhe von Ozeanwellen von der ISS aus. Ich kann 30 dennoch nicht sagen, ob wir die Kurve kriegen*. Ich bin kein Prophet. Es liegt an uns, wir müssen jetzt die richtigen Entscheidungen treffen.

Jutta-Eileen Radix, Irene Meichsner, Lutz Feierabend und Christian Bos, "Jeder sollte die Erde von oben sehen", Interview mit Alexander Gerst, *Kölner Stadt-Anzeiger*, 10./11.01.2015

Glossary (left margin):

- **zerbrechlich** fragile
- **abholzen** to deforest
- **Luftverschmutzung** air pollution
- **achtsam umgehen (mit)** to take proper care (of)
- **größtenteils** to a large extent
- **abschütteln** to shake off
- **Symbolfigur** symbolic figure, symbol, iconic figure, icon
- **Moralapostel** moraliser, upholder of moral standards
- **vermitteln** to convey
- **Umgang** way of dealing
- **driften** to drift
- **Verantwortung tragen** to bear responsibility
- **Raumfahrt** space travel
- **Umweltbeobachtungssatellit** environmental monitoring satellite
- **messen** to measure
- **die Kurve kriegen** (*coll.*) to get things right
- **hoax** trick, deception

Naomi Klein (born in Montreal, Quebec, Canada, in 1970)

M2 Climate Change: Inconvenient Truth or Hoax*?

M2a This Changes Everything: Capitalism vs. the Climate

Naomi Klein

Naomi Klein is a Canadian author, social activist, and filmmaker known for her political analyses and criticism of corporate globalization and of corporate capitalism. The excerpt has been taken from the opening chapter of her latest book, *This Changes Everything: Capitalism vs. the Climate*, a *New York Times* non-fiction bestseller.

 1. Before reading the text, have a look at some quotations that Klein alludes to (cf. ll. 46/47). Paraphrase what Trump and Palin suggest here and hypothesise why they do so.

5. "It is clear that in the early twenty-first century, immediate steps should have been taken to begin a transition to a zero-net-carbon world. Staggeringly, the opposite occurred. At the very time that the urgent need for an energy transition became palpable, world production of greenhouse gases *increased*." (ll. 20-23). **Comment** on the future historian's judgmental remark. In your comment, include knowledge that you have gained from dealing with previous texts and tasks.

Excerpt 1

Meanwhile, climate change was intensifying. In 2010, record-breaking summer heat and fires killed more than 50,000 people in Russia and resulted in more than $15 billion (USD) in damages. The following year, massive floods in Australia affected more than 250,000 people. In 2012, which became known in the United States as the "year without a
5 winter", winter temperature records, including for the highest overnight lows, were shattered* – something that should have been an obvious cause for concern. A summer of unprecedented* heat waves and loss of livestock* and agriculture followed. The "year without a winter" moniker* was misleading, as the warm winter was largely restricted to the United States, but in 2023, the infamous* "year of perpetual summer" lived up to its
10 name, taking 500,000 lives worldwide' and costing nearly $500 billion in losses due to fires, crop failure, and the deaths of livestock and companion animals.

The loss of pet cats and dogs garnered* particular attention among wealthy Westerners, but what was anomalous in 2023 soon became the new normal. Even then, political, business, and religious leaders refused to accept that what lay behind the increasing destruc-
15 tiveness of these disasters was the burning of fossil fuels. More heat in the atmosphere meant more energy had to be dissipated*, manifesting as more powerful storms, bigger deluges*, deeper droughts. It was that simple. But a shadow of ignorance and denial had fallen over people who considered themselves children of the Enlightenment*. It is for this reason that we now know this era as the Period of the Penumbra*.
20 It is clear that in the early twenty-first century, immediate steps should have been taken to begin a transition to a zero-net-carbon* world. Staggeringly*, the opposite occurred. At the very time that the urgent need for an energy transition became palpable*, world production of greenhouse gases *increased*.

Naomi Oreskes and Erik M. Conway, *The Collapse of Western Civilization – A View from the Future*, Columbia University Press, New York 2014, pp. 8/9, © 2014 Columbia University Press. Reprinted with permission of the publisher

to shatter to smash, to destroy
unprecedented [ʌnˈpresidentid] not experienced before
livestock cattle, horses, poultry, and similar animals kept for domestic use but not as pets
moniker name, nickname
infamous notorious
to garner to gather, to receive, to get
to dissipate to spend wastefully
deluge [ˈdeljuːdʒ] a great flood
Enlightenment *cf. vocabulary box*
zero-net-carbon *cf. vocabulary box*
staggeringly amazingly
palpable obvious, noticeable

New luxury towers crowd Sunny Isles Beach, Florida. Miami and its suburbs face a bigger financial risk from flooding in 2050 than any other urban area in the world.

Excerpt 2

The ultimate blow for Western civilization came in a development that, like so many others, had long been discussed but rarely fully assimilated* as a realistic threat: the collapse of the West Antarctica Ice Sheet. Technically, what happened in West Antarctica was not a collapse; the ice sheet did not fall in on itself, and it did not happen all at once. It was more of a rapid disintegration. Post hoc* failure analysis shows that extreme heat in the Northern Hemisphere disrupted* normal patterns of ocean circulation, sending exceptionally warm surface waters into the southern ocean that destabilized the ice sheet from below. As large pieces of ice shelf began to separate from the main ice sheet, removing the bulwark* that had kept the sheet on the Antarctic Peninsula, sea level began to rise rapidly. 10

Social disruption hampered* scientific data-gathering, but some dedicated individuals – realizing the damage could not be stopped – sought, at least, to chronicle* it. Over the course of the next two decades (from 2073 to 2093), approximately 90 percent of the ice sheet broke apart, disintegrated and melted, driving up sea level approximately five meters across most of the globe. Meanwhile, the Greenland Ice Sheet began its own disintegration. As summer melting reached the center of the Greenland Ice Sheet, the east side began to separate from the west. Massive ice breakup ensued*, adding another two meters to mean* global sea level rise. These cryogenic* events were soon referred to as the Great Collapse, although some scholars now use the term more broadly to include the interconnected social, economic, political, and demographic collapse that ensued. 20

Analysts had predicted that an eight-meter sea level rise would dislocate* 10 percent of the global population. Alas*, their estimates proved low: the reality was closer to 20 percent. Although records for this period are incomplete, it is likely that during the Mass Migration 1.5 billion people were displaced around the globe, either directly from the impacts of sea level rise or indirectly from other impacts of climate change, including the secondary dislocation of inland peoples whose towns and villages were overrun by eustatic* refugees. 25

Naomi Oreskes and Erik M. Conway, *The Collapse of Western Civilization – A View from the Future*, Columbia University Press, New York 2014, pp. 29/30, © 2014 Columbia University Press. Reprinted with permission of the publisher

to assimilate to learn and understand thoroughly

post hoc (*Latin*) formulated after the fact, after the event, with the benefit of hindsight
to disrupt to alter or interrupt the normal course or process
bulwark ['bulwək] rampart, barricade
to hamper to prevent the progress of
to chronicle to record in a historical report

to ensue to take place as a result
mean average
cryogenic [ˌkraɪəʊˈdʒenɪk] relating to very low temperatures
to dislocate *here:* to force someone to move from a place or position
Alas! an exclamation of grief or alarm

eustatic relating to global changes in sea level

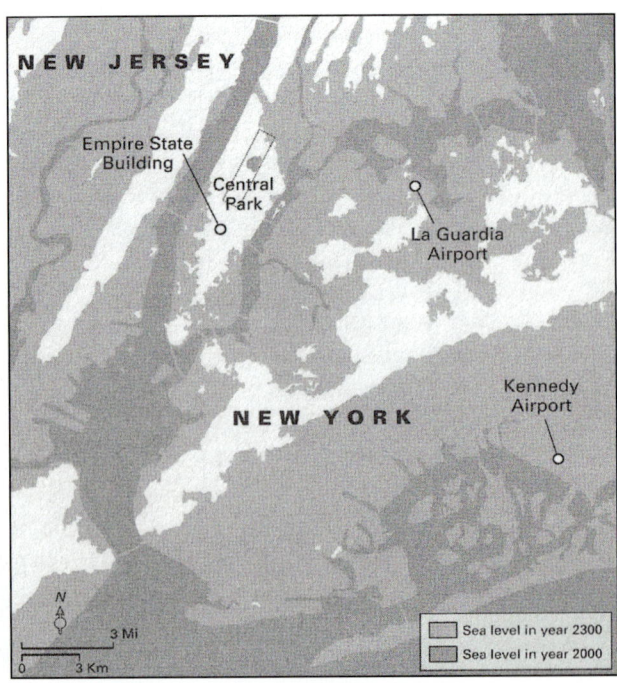

Enlightenment refers to an 18th-century philosophical movement stressing the importance of reason and the critical reappraisal of existing ideas and social institutions (*Aufklärung*).

Penumbra (from Latin *paene* 'almost' and *umbra* 'shadow') normally refers to the outer part of a conical shadow, cast by a celestial body, where the light from the sun is partially blocked – as compared to the umbra, the shadow's darkest, central part, where the light is totally excluded. Here it is used to denote the dark period marked by "a shadow of ignorance and denial" (l. 17), as opposed to the bright period of Enlightenment.

Zero-net-carbon (or **carbon-neutral**) refers to achieving net zero carbon emissions by 'balancing' a certain measured amount of carbon released with an amount of carbon offsets. This assumes that land use change can be designed to take CO_2 out of the carbon cycle. Buying enough carbon credits to make up the difference is even treated as a way to achieving carbon neutral. This, however, is dangerously misleading as there is no such thing as offsetting carbon emissions over the long term.

M 4 Intergovernmental Panel on Climate Change

Attempts at combating climate change have been made at quite a few conferences and summits since the Kyoto Protocol to the UN Framework Convention on Climate Change (UNFCCC) in 1997. Then, 38 nations signed the agreement, for the first time acknowledging global warming as a fact. Meanwhile, there are 191 parties to the Kyoto Protocol and one supranational union, the EU.

In February 2015, when the Intergovernmental Panel on Climate Change (IPCC) held its 41st session in Nairobi, Kenya, Co-Chair Youba Sokona presented the essential points of the Panel's Fifth Assessment Report, written by over 800 scientists from 80 countries. The first part of the report provides the evidence base for key messages (*cf. below*), the second part discloses potential risks, and the third part offers solutions.

1. **State** what evidence the IPCC gives of man's influence on the climate system. Focus on both text and visuals (cf. skills & vocabulary box, p. 43).

2. **Explain** the role of the visuals in showing possible links between mankind and climate change.

3. Go to the IPCC's homepage (http://ipcc.ch > presentations > pdf download) and finish reading the presentation in question. Then prepare a five-minute talk on the risks related to human influence on the climate and the solutions the IPCC offers.

4. Do further research on the Kyoto Protocol and its Doha Amendment as well as on the objective of the 2015 UN Climate Change Conference in Paris. Jot down a few notes required to cope with task no. 5.

5. Finally, stage a formal debate between representatives of the IPCC on the one hand and climate change deniers on the other hand. The topic of the debate is 'Climate change – man-made or natural?'.

ZOOM IN: Information

The **Intergovernmental Panel on Climate Change (IPCC)** is the international body for assessing the science related to climate change. The IPCC was set up in 1988 by the World Meteorological Organization (WMO) and the United Nations Environment Programme (UNEP) to provide policymakers with regular assessments of the scientific basis of climate change, its impacts and future risks, and options for adaptation and mitigation.

Key Messages

Human influence on the climate system is clear. The more we disrupt our climate, the more we risk severe, pervasive* and irreversible impacts. We have the means to limit climate change and build a more prosperous, sustainable future.

5 [It is] extremely likely that human influence has been the dominant cause of warming since the mid-20th century.

pervasive widespread

°C degree Celsius

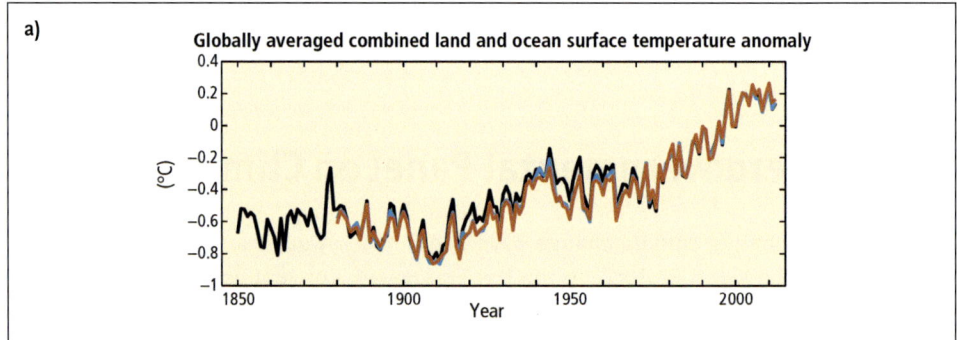

m metre

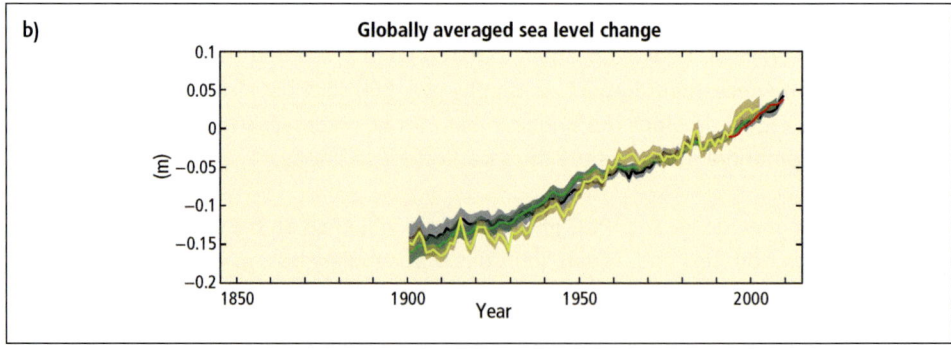

ppm parts per million
ppb parts per billion
CO2 carbon dioxide
CH4 methane
N2O nitrous oxide

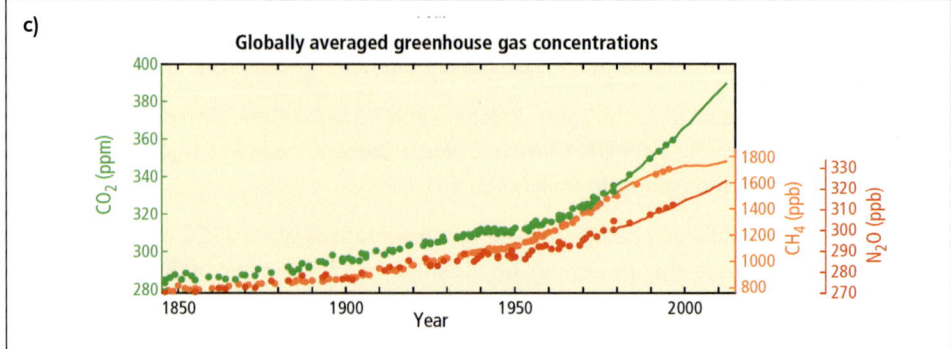

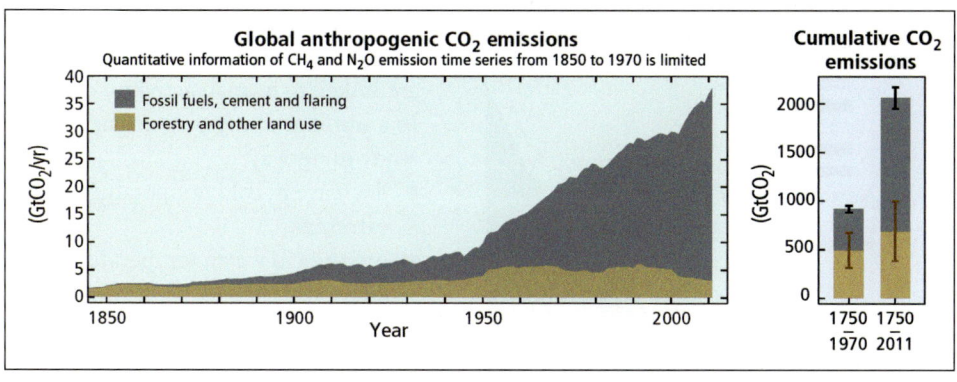

cumulative increasing by successive addition
fossil fuels *here:* fossil-fuel burning
cement *here:* hydraulic cement production
flaring *here:* gas flaring (*Abfackelung*)
GtCO2 gigatonnes of carbon dioxide
yr (per) year

Anthropogenic* GHG* emissions have increased since the preindustrial era, driven largely by economic and population growth.
The atmospheric concentrations of carbon dioxide, methane and nitrous oxide [...] are unprecedented in at least the last 800,000 years.

anthropogenic
[ˌænθrəpəʊˈdʒɛnɪk]
caused by humans
GHG greenhouse gas

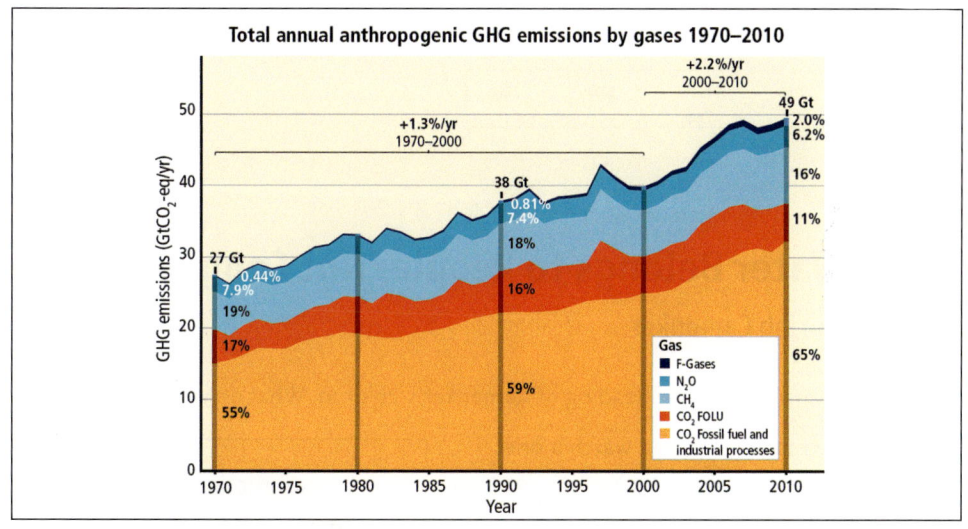

F-Gases man-made fluorinated gases that can stay in the atmosphere for centuries and contribute to a global greenhouse effect
FOLU forestry and other land use

Sources of Emissions
Energy production remains the primary driver of GHG emissions.

35%	24%	21%	14%	6,4%
Energy Sector	Agriculture, forests and other land uses	Industry	Transport	Building Sector

2010 GHG emissions

Oceans absorb most of the heat.
90%+ of the energy that accumulated in the climate system from 1971 and 2010 was absorbed by the oceans. Land temperatures set a record high in 2014 while ocean temperatures continue to climb.

J Joule [dʒuːl] the
standard unit of energy
(1 joule = 1 watt-second)

precipitation *Niederschlag*

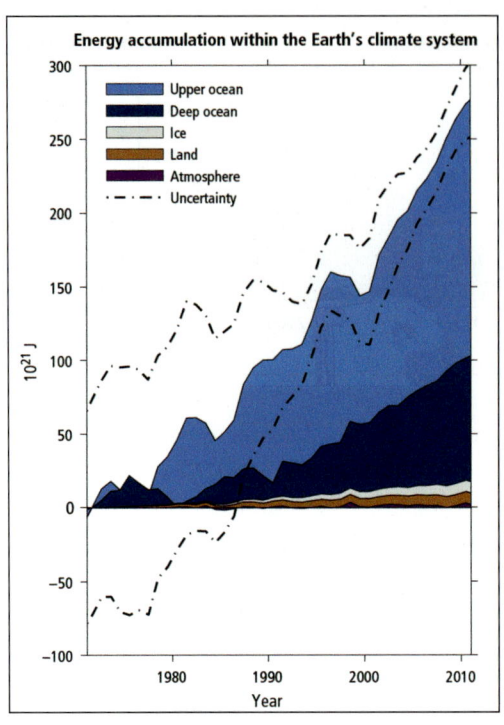

Energy accumulation within the Earth's climate system

Legend:
- Upper ocean
- Deep ocean
- Ice
- Land
- Atmosphere
- Uncertainty

Some changes in extreme weather and
climate events observed since ~1950
are linked to human activity.
In a number of regions, impacts are already underway: 5
- decrease in cold temperature
  extremes
- increase in warm temperature
  extremes
- increase in extreme high sea levels   10
- increase in the number of heavy
  precipitation* events

Youba Sokona, *Presentation of the IPCC Fifth Assessment Report*, http://ipcc.ch, United Nations,
Nairobi, 23.02.2015 [31.05.2015] © Intergovernmental Panel on Climate Change, 2015

M5 Water Belongs to People, Not Companies

Moriah Camenker

1. Brainstorm about the heading of Camenker's column. What do you expect?

2. Before reading the text, watch a brief
commercial advertising Nestlé's *Pure
Life* brand (see Webcode). Which
aspect of the product is emphasised by
which means? Exchange ideas with a
partner.

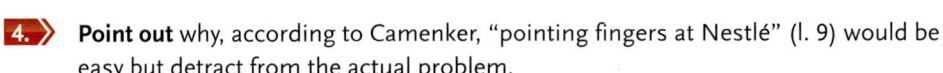

3. Do some research on Nestlé ['nɛslɪ],
the Swiss multinational food and
beverage company. Visualise the princi-
pal points of your research in a word web or mind map (cf. skills pages).

4. **Point out** why, according to Camenker, "pointing fingers at Nestlé" (l. 9) would be
easy but detract from the actual problem.

5. **State** the writer's opinion on the water industry and on water rights (cf. terminology box).

6. **Analyse** by which means she emphasises her opinion. Focus on her choice of
words and line of argument.

7. Who owns water? **Discuss** this question against the backdrop of Camenker's
opinion piece.

ZOOM IN: Information

Water rights

During the California Gold Rush, water was the key to gold mining, so miners worked out a system of 'first dibs' in order to protect their rights. Nowadays, much of the American West, where water supplies are limited and must be allocated sparingly based on the productivity of its use, follows the 'first dibs' rules, while much of the American East follows traditional riparian rights. California follows both.

Prior-appropriation water rights: ('first dibs') the rights which are allotted to those who are 'first in time of use', unconnected to land ownership, and which can be sold or mortgaged like other property.

Riparian water rights: the rights which belong to landowners through whose property a natural watercourse runs to the benefit of such stream for all purposes to which it can be applied.

As California scrambles* to conserve water during a historic drought, one multinational company is continuing to take huge gulps of the state's water for profit. Nestlé Waters North America, a subsidiary* of food and beverage company Nestlé, has been tapping California's groundwater to sell in plastic bottles for its Arrowhead and Pure Life brands*.

5 Essentially, Nestlé has been taking water from the state's natural underground aquifers* and selling it. In a time when Californians are facing emergency mandates* to reduce water usage by 25 percent, it is appalling* Nestlé is still permitted to drill and sell this precious resource.

It would be easy to spend the rest of this column pointing fingers at Nestlé – which, by the

10 way, has a CEO* who once said water is not a basic public right – but that would be ignoring the real problem. We should really be blaming a governmental system that failed to regulate and protect California's natural resources.

Until recently, California had no existing laws that regulate how much water can be pumped from underground aquifers, which have been gradually drying up across the

15 state.

Not only could California landowners drill as much groundwater as they wanted, but also they weren't usually required to disclose* the amount of water they were taking. Even when they did report the numbers, public access to the records is highly restricted. Recent laws that are intended to correct this issue may not even take effect until 2040.

20 Nestlé easily benefits from this regulatory oversight*. It has a longstanding partnership with the Morongo Band of Mission Indians and pumps water from underground wells on the tribe's reservation. Basically, Nestlé can take as much water as it can afford, even while California residents face water rationing.

This is pretty ridiculous considering the fact that groundwater provides almost 60 percent

25 of the state's water supply during a drought year. It is astounding state officials have done so little to preserve these valuable underground aquifers and instead have allowed a corporation to lay claim to them.

Nestlé, the largest producer of bottled water in the country, used 705 million gallons* of water from California last year. The company uses a California national forest as one of its

30 water sources, and it is currently being investigated by the U.S. Forest Service for using an expired* permit. The investigation would be promising news if it had actually occurred when the permit expired, which was in 1988.

It is disappointing and completely unacceptable that both Nestlé and the forest officials ignored the expired permit for nearly three decades. By not renewing the permit, Nestlé

35 continued its operations without having to undergo an environmental review, which is

to scramble to struggle frantically in order to get something
subsidiary a company whose controlling interest is owned by another company
Arrowhead, Pure Life brand names of bottled water produced by Nestlé Waters North America
aquifer ['ækwɪfə] an underground layer of sand, gravel, or porous rock that collects water and holds it like a sponge
mandate official order
appalling [ə'pɔːlɪŋ] disgusting
CEO (chief executive officer) the head of a company, the person with the most authority in a company
to disclose to make known
oversight an unintentional mistake

gallon a unit of volume, used in liquid measure (1 U.S. gallon = 3.785 litres)

expired having come to an end

ultimately in the end

wary on guard, watchful

incredibly important when you're pumping water from a national forest. This responsibility should have been handled, yet officials are only now deciding to "investigate" the issue.

It is ultimately* up to the people of California to convince their government to stand up for their resources, but it is time for all of us to think about how the bottled water industry affects our environment. 40

According to the National Resources Defense Council, more than half of all Americans drink bottled water, and about a third drink it regularly.

As consumers, we need to be wary* of buying into such a wasteful and misleading industry that sells a product that has never been proven to be safer or purer than tap water. 45

This industry does not deserve to have unchecked access to our country's water supply.

California's water should remain with the people of California, not with a company that exploits the environment to sell glorified tap water.

States nationwide should learn from California's mistakes and do more to protect this precious resource. 50

Water is the public's right, not a corporation's right.

Hopefully it will start to be treated that way.

Moriah Camenker, "Water Belongs to People, Not Companies", www.alligator.org, 13.04.2015 [31.05.2015]
© The Independent Florida Alligator, Gainesville, FL

8. ›› Here in Germany, we take clean water for granted. We turn on the tap and there it is. However, in other parts of the world, clean, safe water is scarce. According to the United Nations World Health Organisation (WHO), only half of the world's population have tap water in their homes or on their grounds.
Do further research on the global water crisis with the aim of understanding why "water is to the twenty-first century what oil was to the twentieth" (*Fortune*, 15 May 2000). In your research, include the role of globally operating companies in investing in water overseas.

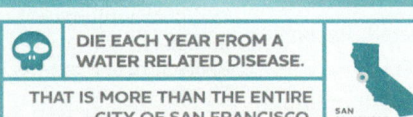

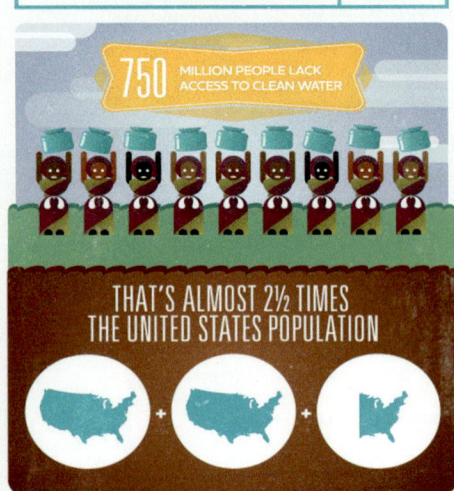

Lake Oroville - July 20, 2011

Then-and-now photographs of California's drought

Lake Oroville - January 16, 2014

M6 Drill or Drop?

M6a Promised Land

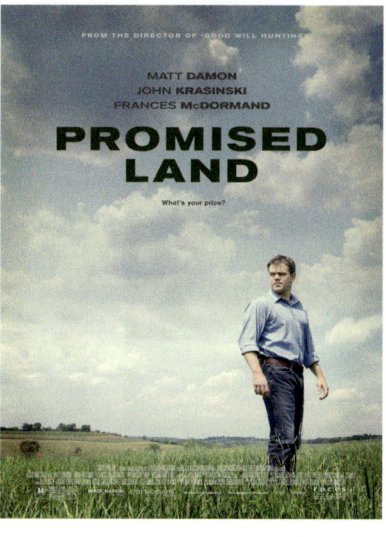

Promised Land (released in December 2012) is an American film directed by Gus Van Sant and starring Matt Damon and John Krasinski. Damon and Krasinski also wrote the screenplay, which is based on a story by Dave Eggers (cf. M4, p. 14). *Promised Land* centres around Steve Butler (performed by Damon), a salesman who, on behalf of the energy corporation he works with, visits a small rural town in order to buy mineral rights* from the financially distressed local farmers.

mineral rights *cf.* terminology box

In the scene below, Dustin Noble (performed by Krasinski), who pretends to be an environmentalist trying to protect habitats and wildlife, explains to a class of ten-year-olds how hydraulic fracturing, or fracking, works.

1. Before reading, have a close look at the film poster and think about the film title. What kind of mood do both evoke? So what do you expect the film to zoom in on?

2. **Describe** the fracking method, as explained by Dustin Noble.

3. **Illustrate** how Dustin eventually succeeds in making the youngsters understand the impact of drilling for natural gas under their family farm's land. Focus on his language and modus operandi*.

modus operandi (*Latin*) a person's method of working

4. Alice, the 5th-graders' teacher, seems to increasingly feel ill at ease during that scene. What about you? **Discuss** whether Dustin's experiment is an appropriate means to an end.

47 INT. ROOM – DAY

We come up on an indecipherable* background. A greyish wall. After a beat: Dustin enters from out of frame* as we pull out to reveal … a black board.

DUSTIN

5 Good morning, everyone! My name is Dustin!

We immediately reveal … a classroom of kids.

KIDS

Hi Dustin!!!

As we pull out more we see that in front of him is a brown bag of unknown supplies and on the
10 *floor is a large box. He's talking to Alice's 5th grade* class. She stands off to the side, admiring.*

DUSTIN

How many of you live on a farm?

Almost all the hands go up.

DUSTIN

15 Alright!

From behind the desk he pulls up a large clear bag full of dirt and places it on the table. He then reaches into the bag and pulls out a few toy figures of cows and horses.

DUSTIN

Now, let's say THIS is your farm!

20 5TH GRADER

indecipherable [ˌɪndɪˈsaɪfərəbl] impossible to recognize
frame the bounded area of a visual image

5th grade (in the U.S.) the fifth year of school, when children are ten or eleven years old

Geesh! [dʒiːʃ] *acronym meaning* Gee, shit happens!

In Spectro Peculium! (*Latin*) Let's imagine it's a cattle farm! (*In ancient Rome,* **peculium** *was property mainly consisting of* **pecus**, *cattle.*)
Poof! exclamation used to indicate a sudden disappearance
Whew! [hwjuː] a whistling exclamation expressing relief

wary cautious, not showing complete trust in someone who could be dangerous or cause trouble, on guard

to puncture to pierce with a pointed object

That's a bag of dirt!
DUSTIN
I know, I know! Geesh*! Thought 5th graders were supposed to have imaginations. (*He smiles*) Ok, how about this!
He picks up a pencil and waves it over the bag of dirt.   25
DUSTIN
In Spectro Peculium*! Poof*! Now it's a farm! Ok?
The kids laugh.
DUSTIN
Whew*! Thank God for Harry Potter!   30
[...]

49 INT. CLASSROOM – DAY
DUSTIN
And this ...
From behind the desk he pulls up a big clear Tupperware container and pours in a large bottle of 35
water.
DUSTIN
And THIS is all the water in town! The water you drink, the water the cows drink, the water your puppies and kittens drink and all the water in the river for the fish.
Alice looks at him warily*, a bit perplexed.   40
DUSTIN
Now let me show you what happened one day in my hometown, in a state called Nebraska, when this company GLOBAL tried drilling for natural gas.
He holds the bag over the container of water. Suddenly he begins puncturing* the bottom of the bag with a pencil.   45
DUSTIN
See, they wanted to drill into the land, like this.
The kids laugh at the rather destructive action. Little bits of dirt start falling into the water.
DUSTIN
But hold on, hold on! That's not all! In order to do all that drilling they need to use ...   50
From the brown paper bag he pulls out 5 or 6 bottles of home cleaning products.
DUSTIN
Chemicals! Now these chemicals that they use seem harmless when they're contained right? In fact a lot of the bad stuff up there you can find right here in the bottles under your sink at home. But they don't use one chemical at a time. They use all of them.   55

Dustin starts to pour all the products into the bag. Alice pulls away a little from the smell. After a moment, a gross concoction* of dark ooze* starts dripping from the bag.

KIDS

Ewwwww*!

60 *They're all a bit horrified.*

[...]

52 INT. CLASSROOM – DAY

DUSTIN

Now ...

65 *He reaches into the box and pulls out a lighter. A few gasps.*

KIDS

Whoa.

ALICE

Oh, I don't think ...

70 DUSTIN

It's ok.

Dustin lowers the lighter to the discolored water. After a moment, it ignites*! Then burns gently.

KIDS

Whoa*!!!!!

75 *They all cheer.*

[...]

54 INT. CLASSROOM – DAY

The kids are cheering.

DUSTIN

80 Why are you cheering?

KIDS

It's so cool!

DUSTIN

But that's the water you drink.

85 KIDS

Oh yeah./I guess.

Needing a big finish, Dustin looks around the room and sees ... on the windowsill is an aquarium. Inside is a very unlucky turtle.

DUSTIN

90 What's the turtle's name?

KIDS

Trigger!

DUSTIN

Does his water look like it's as clean as this water?

95 *A few kids answer quietly ...*

KIDS

No. No way.

Silence. In a flash*, Dustin has pulled the turtle out and is back in front of the flames.

DUSTIN

100 Well, let's see if Trigger here can survive in his new home.

BLOODCURDLING* SCREAMS FROM THE KIDS!! ... and Alice. Dustin stops. He's given the greatest presentation ever.

Promised Land, screenplay by John Krasinki and Matt Damon, story by Dave Eggers, 2012 www.screenplaydb.com [31.05.2015]

---

a gross concoction a disgusting mixture
ooze soft mud or slime
Ewwwww! ['iːuː] exclamation showing great disgust or nausea

to ignite to catch fire

Whoa! [wəʊ] exclamation expressing surprise and astonishment

in a flash very quickly

bloodcurdling causing great horror, terrifying

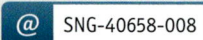 SNG-40658-008

5. Now watch the film trailer on *YouTube* (see Webcode) and double-check your expectations from task 1. Does the mood of the film poster and the title correspond with the one evoked by the highly condensed trailer?

ZOOM IN: Information

Mineral rights

In the U.S., mineral rights can be sold or conveyed separately from property rights. As a result, owning a piece of land does not necessarily mean you also own the rights to the minerals beneath it.

A mineral owner has the right to extract and use minerals found beneath the surface of a particular piece of land. What minerals are included depends on the terms of the specific conveyance (the document according to which someone bought or sold the rights). The conveyance might include all the minerals under the land, or be limited to specified minerals.

In areas where mineral exploitation is common, whether or not you own the minerals under your land might be a real concern. For example, if your property is in an area where natural gas drilling is prevalent, if you just own the land but not the minerals underneath, the mineral owner can excavate a mine on your property, build roadways or make other improvements necessary to facilitate the mineral extraction.

Red Hawk Elementary School

Fracking operation in Erie, Colorado

M 6b What Exactly Is Fracking?

1. In simple terms, **describe** the fracking process, as shown in the illustration.

2. Briefly **explain** why this process gives rise to concerns. In your explanation, also include aspects of Dustin Noble's corresponding experiment (*cf. M 6a*).

3. In case you have not yet fully understood how fracking works, watch an animated representation of the whole process (see Webcode).

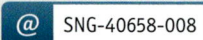 SNG-40658-009

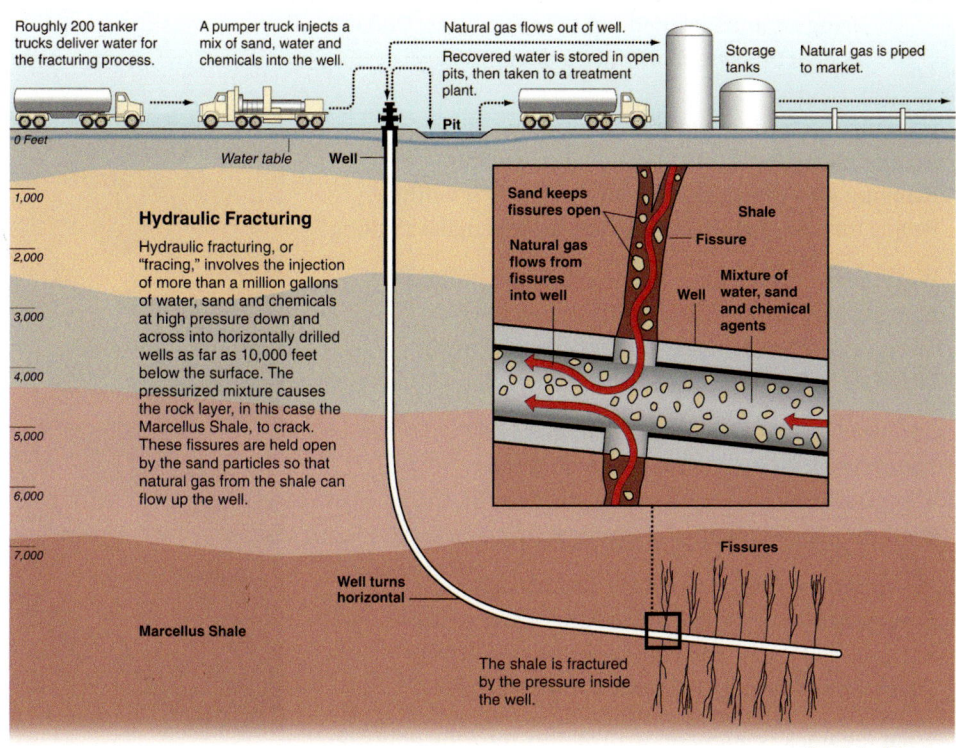

Roughly 200 tanker trucks deliver water for the fracturing process.

A pumper truck injects a mix of sand, water and chemicals into the well.

Natural gas flows out of well.

Recovered water is stored in open pits, then taken to a treatment plant.

Storage tanks

Natural gas is piped to market.

Pit

0 Feet

Water table   Well

1,000

2,000

3,000

4,000

5,000

6,000

7,000

Hydraulic Fracturing

Hydraulic fracturing, or "fracing," involves the injection of more than a million gallons of water, sand and chemicals at high pressure down and across into horizontally drilled wells as far as 10,000 feet below the surface. The pressurized mixture causes the rock layer, in this case the Marcellus Shale, to crack. These fissures are held open by the sand particles so that natural gas from the shale can flow up the well.

Sand keeps fissures open

Natural gas flows from fissures into well

Shale

Fissure

Well

Mixture of water, sand and chemical agents

Marcellus Shale

Well turns horizontal

Fissures

The shale is fractured by the pressure inside the well.

Graphic by Al Granberg

hydraulic [haɪˈdrɒlɪk] operated by pressure transmitted through a pipe by a liquid, such as water or oil
fracturing the characteristic manner in which a mineral breaks, cracks or splits
pit a large, deep opening in the ground
fissure [ˈfɪʃə] a long, narrow crack or cleft
shale a sedimentary rock formed by the deposition of successive layers of clay
Marcellus Shale a type of marine sedimentary rock found in eastern North America

M7 My Water's on Fire Tonight (The Fracking Song)

"My Water's on Fire Tonight" (The Fracking Song) is a 2011 American song and accompanying music video about the environmental and public health effects of fracking. David Holmes, who sings the song with Andrew Bean, used data collected by the investigative journalism group *ProPublica* to write the song.

1. ⟫ Before dealing with the fracking song, watch an energy lobby advert on *YouTube* (see Webcode). Remember to take notes on its overall message. Compare your notes with those of a partner and help each other to close any potential gaps. Then introduce "the world's newest energy superpower" to the class.

2. ⟫ Read the lyrics of the fracking song and the annotations, then watch the music video (see Webcode). Swap ideas with a partner on whether you would "like" the song on *Facebook* or not.

3. ⟫ **Write** a prose **summary** of the song.

4. ⟫ Rapping is spoken or chanted rhyming lyrics performed in time to a beat. Rappers use literary techniques such as similes or metaphors, alliteration and other forms of wordplay. Their vocabulary is often complex, their message frequently socio-critical. **Examine** the fracking song with regard to these features.

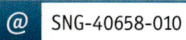
@ SNG-40658-010

@ SNG-40658-011

5. Upon its release in 2011, the song and video received a lot of media attention for using an unusual medium to report news. **Evaluate** whether a music video can be as effective and efficient as a documentary.

Fracking is a form of natural gas drilling
An alternative to oil 'cause the oil kept spilling
Bringing jobs to small towns so everybody's willing
People turn on their lights and the drillers make a killing

Water goes into the pipe, the pipe into the ground
The pressure creates fissures 7,000 feet down
The cracks release the gas that powers your town
That well is fracked ... Yeah, totally fracked

But there's more in the water than just H2O
Toxic chemicals help to make the fluid flow
With names like benzene and formaldehyde
You better keep 'em far away from the water supply

The drillers say the fissures are a mile below
The groundwater pumped into American homes
But don't tell it to the residents of Sublette Wy-O*
That water's fracked ... We're talking Benzene ...

Fracking hot: man sets tap water on fire

What the frack is going on with all this fracking going on
I think we need some facts to come to light
I know we want our energy but nothing ever comes for free
I think my water's on fire tonight

So it all goes back to 2005
Bush said gas drillers didn't have to comply*
with the Safe Drinking Water Act*, before too long
It was "frack, baby, frack" until the break of dawn.

With the EPA* out it was up to the states
But they didn't have the money to investigate
Sick people couldn't prove fracking was to blame
All the while water wells were going up in flames

'Cause it's hard to contain all the methane released
It can get into the air, it can get into the streams.
It's a greenhouse gas, worse than CO2
Fracking done wrong could lead to climate change too

Now it's not that drillers should never be fracking
But the current regulation is severely lacking
Reduce the toxins, contain the gas and wastewater
And the people won't get sick and the planet won't get hotter

What the frack is going on with all this fracking going on
I think we need some facts to come to light
I know we want our energy but nothing ever comes for free
I think my water's on fire tonight

"The Fracking Song (My Water's on Fire Tonight)", vocals and lyrics by David Holmes and Niel Bekker, www.propublica.org, 12.05.2011 [31.05.2015]

In July 2008, a hydrologist dropped a plastic-sampling pipe 300 feet down a water well in rural **Sublette County, Wyoming**, and pulled up a load of brown oily water with a foul smell. Tests showed it contained **benzene**, a chemical believed to cause aplastic anemia and leukemia, in a concentration 1,500 times the level safe for human consumption. The results sent shockwaves through the energy industry and state and federal regulatory agencies.
to comply (with) to act in accordance with a rule or law
Safe Drinking Water Act, EPA *cf. terminology box*

5

10

15

20

25

30

35

40

The **Safe Drinking Water Act** was established to protect the quality of drinking water in the U.S. This law focuses on all waters actually or potentially designed for drinking use, whether from above ground or underground sources. The Act authorises the U.S. Environmental Protection Agency (**EPA**) to establish minimum standards to protect tap water and requires all owners or operators of public water systems to comply with these primary (health-related) standards. Under the Act, the EPA also establishes minimum standards for state programs to protect underground sources of drinking water from endangerment by underground injection of fluids.

EPA, "Summary of the Safe Drinking Water Act", www.epa.gov [31.05.2015]

However, the **2005 Bush-Cheney Energy Policy Act** exempted (excused) hydraulic fracturing from the Safe Drinking Water Act.

6. ▷ Before tackling the final task on fracking, look at British artist Robin Rutherford's painting "Energy Fracked". **Describe** the painting's colour gradient (*Farbverlauf*) and arrangement as well as its shape, and establish a connection to its title.

Robin Rutherford, "Energy fracked"

7. ▷ Finally yet importantly, let us examine what must be taken into consideration when deciding whether fracking is a method society should come to rely upon. In the table below, you will find some arguments frequently put forward in favour of fracking. Against the backdrop of what you have learned so far, complete the table by inserting some of its disadvantages or dangers.

PROS	CONS
Urgent need for fuel Since the world's supplies of oil and gas are decreasing, finding new methods becomes more and more urgent. Therefore, fracking will persist until a true replacement fuel is found.	
Better air quality By using natural gas instead of coal to generate electricity, carbon dioxide emissions are reduced significantly, which diminishes air pollution.	

PROS	CONS
Less dependency on foreign oil Fracking reduces the dependency on foreign oil. In view of a growing population and political problems in securing a reliable oil supply, uncovering domestic sources is vitally important.	
Lower taxes Fracking is more lucrative than conventional methods because of the industry-friendly tax system in most U.S. states (cf. cartoon).	
Profitable return on investment Drilling for oil or gas by means of fracking is cheaper than conventional methods, thus maximising the return on investments (*Kapitalerträge*).	
...	

M 8   GM: What Exactly Are We Talking about?

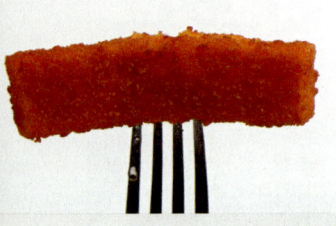

canola *Raps*
dairy products milk products

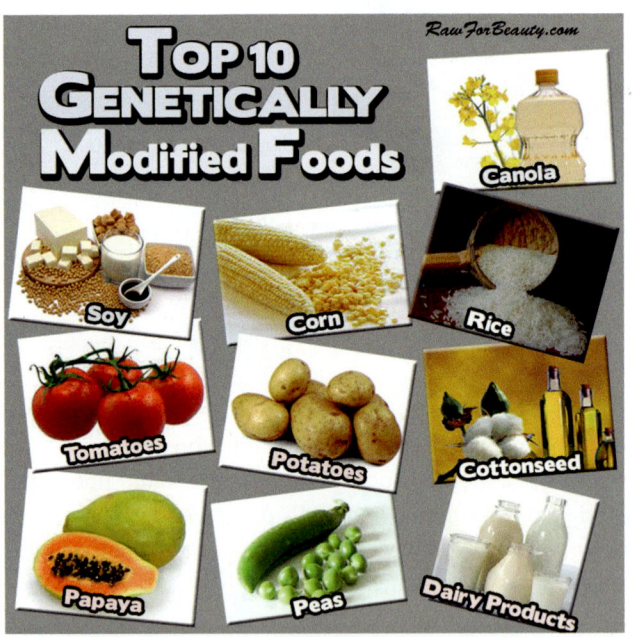

What type of fish was that again? Is there any fish in it? Difficult to tell and it does not really matter. You simply cannot be sure of what you are eating nowadays. When you go to the supermarket or eat out, for example, do you really know which foods are most likely to be genetically modified (GM) or contain ingredients that are? Since the 1990s, world agriculture and food production have undergone the most radical transformation in history. With little public awareness, genetically modified organisms (GMO) have come to dominate both global agriculture and supermarket shelf space. Leaving aside the question of whether they are good or bad for a moment, what exactly are GMOs, and which foods are they in?

1. ⟩ If you had the free choice, would you eat chips or mashed potatoes made from GM potatoes or pasta with *sauce bolognese* from GM tomatoes? Exchange views with a partner.

2. ⟩ With reference to the text, **point out** which type of GMO gives rise to concern, and why.

State why the authors compare gene transfer technology to a cut-and-paste operation and briefly **describe** that operation.

 Explain the conceptual difference between "modifying" and "enhancing" genetic material.

For thousands of years, humans have been genetically enhancing* other organisms through the practice of selective breeding*. Look around you: the sweet corn and seedless watermelons at the supermarket, the purebred* dogs at the park, and your neighbor's prize rosebush are all examples of how humans have selectively enhanced desirable traits
5 in other living things.

The type of genetic enhancement that generates the most concern goes a step beyond selective breeding, however. Technology now allows us to transfer genes between organisms. For example, the tomato plant's beetle resistance relies on a gene from a bacterium (*Bacillus thuringiensis*), which scientists inserted into the tomato plant's genome*. This
10 gene, called *cry1Ac*, encodes a protein that is poisonous to certain types of insects, including the beetle.

> **to enhance** to intensify or increase in quality, value, power, etc.
> **selective breeding** the process by which humans breed animals and plants for particular traits
> **purebred** a cultivated variety of an animal species
> **genome** an organism's genetic material

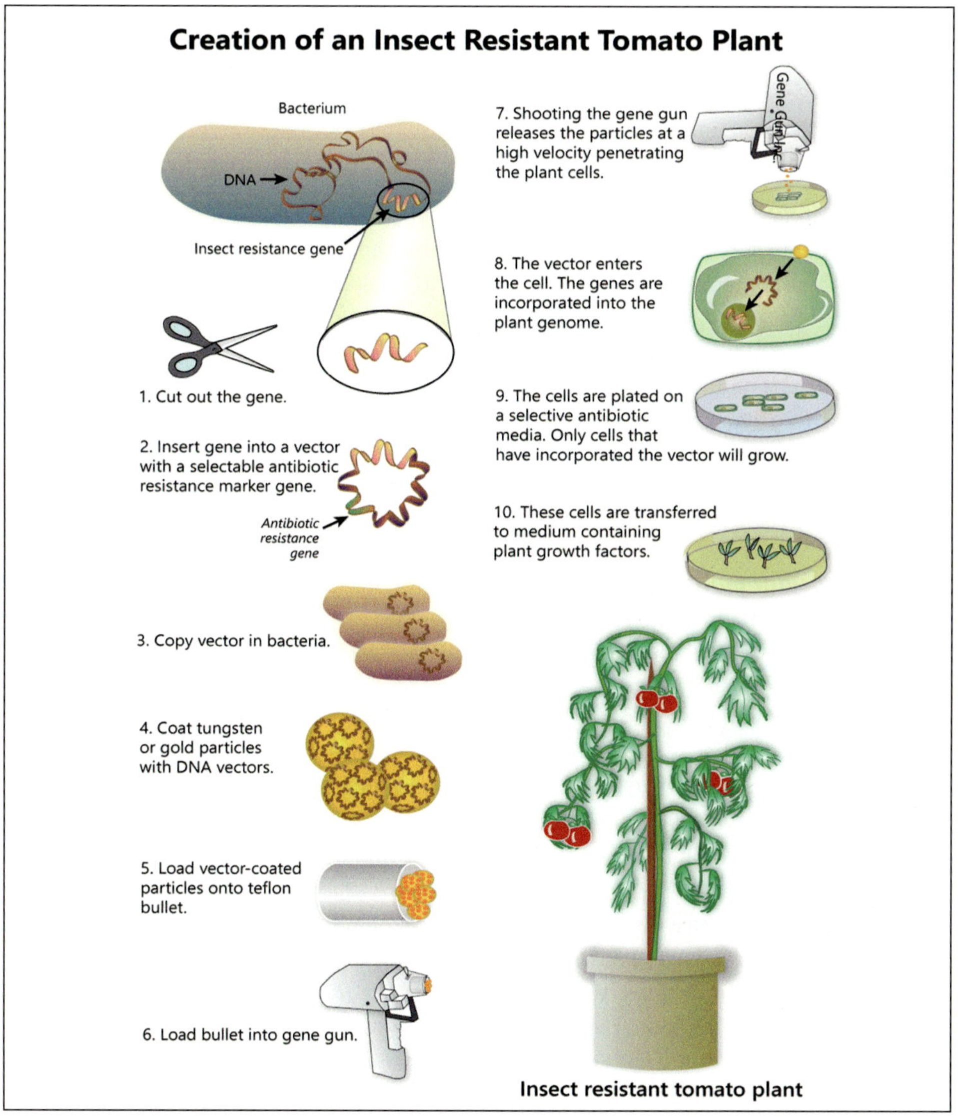

Creation of an Insect Resistant Tomato Plant

Bacterium

DNA →

Insect resistance gene

1. Cut out the gene.

2. Insert gene into a vector with a selectable antibiotic resistance marker gene.

Antibiotic resistance gene →

3. Copy vector in bacteria.

4. Coat tungsten or gold particles with DNA vectors.

5. Load vector-coated particles onto teflon bullet.

6. Load bullet into gene gun.

7. Shooting the gene gun releases the particles at a high velocity penetrating the plant cells.

Gene Gun

8. The vector enters the cell. The genes are incorporated into the plant genome.

9. The cells are plated on a selective antibiotic media. Only cells that have incorporated the vector will grow.

10. These cells are transferred to medium containing plant growth factors.

Insect resistant tomato plant

> **vector** an agent by means of which a fragment of foreign DNA is inserted into a host cell to produce a gene clone in genetic engineering
> **to coat** to cover the surface of
> **tungsten** ['tʌŋstən] a heavy grey-white element having a high melting point
> **velocity** rapidity or speed of motion
> **to incoporate** to cause to merge into a united whole

sophisticated very complex or complicated

How is this done? Gene transfer technology is simply a sophisticated* version of a cut-and-paste operation. Once the desired gene is identified in the native organism's genome, it can be cut out, transferred to the target plant, and pasted into its genome.

University of Utah, "Genetically Modified Foods", http://learn.genetics.utah.edu [31.05.2015]

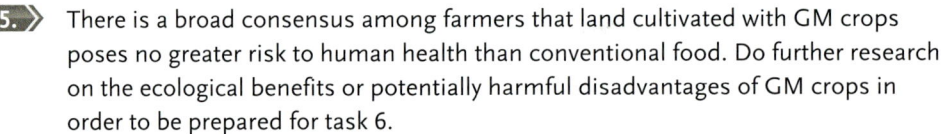

ZOOM IN: Information

Difference between genetically modified (GM) and genetically engineered (GE):

GM describes any type of genetic modification, whether by high-tech, modern genetic engineering or by long-time, traditional plant-breeding methods.

GE describes the high-tech methods used in recent decades to incorporate genes directly into an organism. The only way scientists can transfer genes between organisms that are not sexually compatible is to use recombinant (produced by the combining of genetic material from more than one origin) DNA techniques. The plants that result do not occur in nature; they have been genetically engineered by human intervention and manipulation.

5. ➤➤ There is a broad consensus among farmers that land cultivated with GM crops poses no greater risk to human health than conventional food. Do further research on the ecological benefits or potentially harmful disadvantages of GM crops in order to be prepared for task 6.

6. ➤➤ What would you do in the following situation? In groups of four, agree on a common position and collect arguments supporting that position. Then prepare to slip into the role of the farmer and stand up and defend your decision.
You are a tomato farmer whose crops are threatened by a persistent species of beetle. Each year, you spend large sums of money for pesticides to protect your crops. A biotechnology company introduces a new strain of tomato plant that produces a natural pesticide, making it resistant to the beetle. By switching to this new strain, you could avoid both the beetle and the chemical pesticides traditionally needed to fight it.

ZOOM IN: Skills

Defending your point of view or decision

- Start by introducing yourself, the reason why you are speaking out, and what you want to achieve, e.g. *My name is …/I'm a …/You may have wondered why I've decided to …/I've recently been criticised for my decision to …/I would like to explain to you why …/… justify my choice …*
- Continue by anticipating possible arguments of your critics, e.g. *Opponents/supporters of … argue that …/Obviously, a lot of people (seem to) think that …/I find it hard to believe that …/It is by no means certain that …*
- Express your opinion by referring to your longstanding experience in the field, e.g. *Based on my experience, …/I must say that, given the experiences of the last years, …/…, given everything I have learned, …/Let me give you a practical/real-world example: …/From my point of view as a …, …/There is evidence that …/This proves that …*
- Conclude by summarising your point of view, e.g. *To put it in a nutshell, …/After weighing the pros and cons, I've come to the conclusion that …/The result of this is that …/Last but not least, I'd like to repeat once again that …*

7. Collect data about the American biotech corporation *Monsanto* and present your findings to your class.

8. "I personally would agree to the genetic modification of foods if ...". Complete the sentence with at least three arguments.

A genetically engineered kiwi-orange

Hundreds of people participated in the March against *Monsanto* on 24 May 2014 protesting against genetically engineered foods.

M9 Perfect People, Perfect Foods?

Peter James

Peter James is a best-selling British writer of crime fiction. In this excerpt from his novel *Perfect People*, Timon Cort, a young disciple*, is studying the Law of the Disciples of the Third Millennium before he is allowed to come down from the Rockies to perform the Grand Rite of Passage. This rite includes killing in the name of the Lord so-called 'designer babies', i. e. genetically enhanced children that the sect members view as Satan's progeny*.

disciple [dɪ'saɪpl] a follower or student, e. g. the Twelve Apostles are also referred to as the Twelve Disciples
progeny ['prɒdʒəni] offspring, children
chatter idle, trivial talk

to profess to affirm belief in

1. "Guard what has been entrusted to your care. Turn away from Godless chatter* and the opposing ideas of what is falsely called knowledge, which some have professed* and in so doing have wandered from the faith." (ll. 32 – 34). Make an educated guess about what this quotation from the Law of the Disciples discloses about the sect's attitude towards knowledge and science.

2. **Point out** what stance Cort takes on the issue of science in general and on GE foods in particular.

3. Read the definition of the term 'Creationism' below. Then **examine** to what extent creationist ideas can be discovered in the excerpt. Find and **explain** them.

4. The WHO estimates that over a billion people suffer from hunger worldwide. Put yourself in the shoes of a biology student (with a focus on genetics). Contradict the disciple by arguing that global hunger can be fought with the help of genetically altered plants.

Peter James (born in Brighton, UK, in 1948)

sewer an artificial, usually underground conduit for carrying off sewage or rainwater

mutant *here:* deformed, freak, abnormal

vanity excessive pride in oneself

to seduce to lead astray from duty or faith

bubonic plague *Beulenpest*

to choke up to block up, to have difficulty in breathing
St Paul to Timothy Epistle of Paul the Apostle to Timothy, a New Testament book containing advice on pastoral matters
to guard to protect
tract a leaflet or pamphlet containing a declaration put out by a religious or political group

Mountain air is different to any other kind of air that you can find on this planet. Mountain air doesn't have all that shit that you have to breathe in.

Down below it is just one big sewer*, my friend, and I'm not just talking about the air. Hasn't always been that way, of course. And one day it's going to be all back to how it was. You'll be able to walk the streets of cities and smell flowers. ⁵

Seriously, when was the last time you smelled flowers in a city?

Maybe in a park, but only if the park was big and the flowers had a strong enough scent. And to have a strong enough scent they'd probably been genetically modified.

We can't keep our hands off anything, can't we? I tell you something, you walk in some of those supermarket places, they've got berries the size of apples, apples the size of melons ¹⁰ and those tomatoes, you know the ones I mean, those like big, mutant* things – they have pig genes in them, to give them their colour, to keep them riper longer, but you don't see that on the label.

I tell you, my friend, you step down off the mountain and you walk in the sewers of the valleys and plains, you're stepping into a world you think you might know, but you don't, ¹⁵ trust me, you do not know any of it. Like, get this – there's a big burger chain, a national chain and they're mixing polyester into the bread in their buns – to make them puff out. They're making you eat polyester and all the time you are thinking, hey, bread that looks this good must be doing me good!

That's how cynical scientists are, my friend. ²⁰

You know what science is really about? Scientists pretend it is about knowledge, but the truth is that it is partially about power and about death, but mostly it is about vanity* and greed. People don't invent things for the greater good. They invent them to satisfy their egos.

Everyone is being seduced* by science. All the world leaders. They're hoping science will ²⁵ find a cure for AIDS, forgetting science caused it in the first place. Scientists cured bubonic plague* and smallpox, but what did that do for the human race? Overpopulation.

The Lord has his own way of dealing with overpopulation. He had the balance of nature just fine, until scientists came along and messed it all up.

And think about this, my friend, next time you take a walk down there in the sewers and ³⁰ feel your lungs getting all choked up*. Who is responsible? God or scientists?

Just remember the words of St Paul to Timothy*. 'Guard* what has been entrusted to your care. Turn away from Godless chatter and the opposing ideas of what is falsely called knowledge, which some have professed and in so doing have wandered from the faith.'

Here endeth the 17th Tract* of the 4th Level of the Law of the Disciples of the Third Millen- ³⁵ nium.

Peter James, *Perfect People*, Pan, London 2011, pp. 182/183

ZOOM IN: Information

Creationism is the doctrine that
- matter and all things were created by an omnipotent Creator and did not evolve or develop over time;
- the true story of the creation of the universe is the one recounted in the Bible, especially in the first chapter of Genesis;
- God immediately creates out of nothing a new human soul for each individual born.

M10 Stop TTIP & CETA

STOP TTIP is a European alliance of more than 250 organisations, whose citizens' initiative against TTIP (Transatlantic Trade and Investment Partnership) and CETA (Comprehensive Economic and Trade Agreement) was not accepted in the EU Commission in Brussels. As the organisers consider the Commission's decision to be judicially wrong, they have decided to refer the case to the European Court of Justice. In the meantime, they are conducting the citizens' initiative on a self-organising basis, collecting signatures from supporters all over Europe. Below, you will find an extract from the initiative's leaflet distributed on 18 April 2015.

The European Parliament votes on a TTIP resolution on 28 April 2015.

1. Before dealing with the initiative's concerns, briefly **describe** the map representing current labelling requirements for GM foods worldwide.

2. Against the backdrop of TTIP and CETA (cf. text below), **explain** the effects that the lack of mandatory (obligatory) labelling in the U.S. and Canada will have on the production and sale of GE foods in Europe.

3. Imagine you are an exchange student at a high school in the Canadian prairie province of Saskatchewan [səˈskætʃəwɑːn]. Your classmates over there cannot understand the European commotion surrounding CETA and TTIP. Explain to them the gist of the European concerns, and **outline** the reasons why the citizens' initiative is opposed to the two trade and investment agreements. Mediate in English (cf. skills box, p. 26).

4. Would you have signed the initiative if someone had handed you the leaflet in the pedestrian zone of your city, giving you background information and illustrating some of the reasons for opposing the agreements? **Justify** your answer.

Gute Gründe gegen TTIP und CETA

Derzeit verhandeln die EU und die USA den transatlantischen Handels- und Investitionsvertrag TTIP. CETA, ein ähnliches Abkommen mit Kanada, steht vor der Ratifizierung*. Diese Abkommen drohen, Demokratie und Rechtsstaat*, Umwelt- und Verbrau-
5 cherschutz* zugunsten von Wirtschaftsinteressen auszuhebeln*. Profitieren werden

Ratifizierung ratification
Rechtsstaat constitutional state
Verbraucherschutz consumer protection
aushebeln to overrule, to make null and void

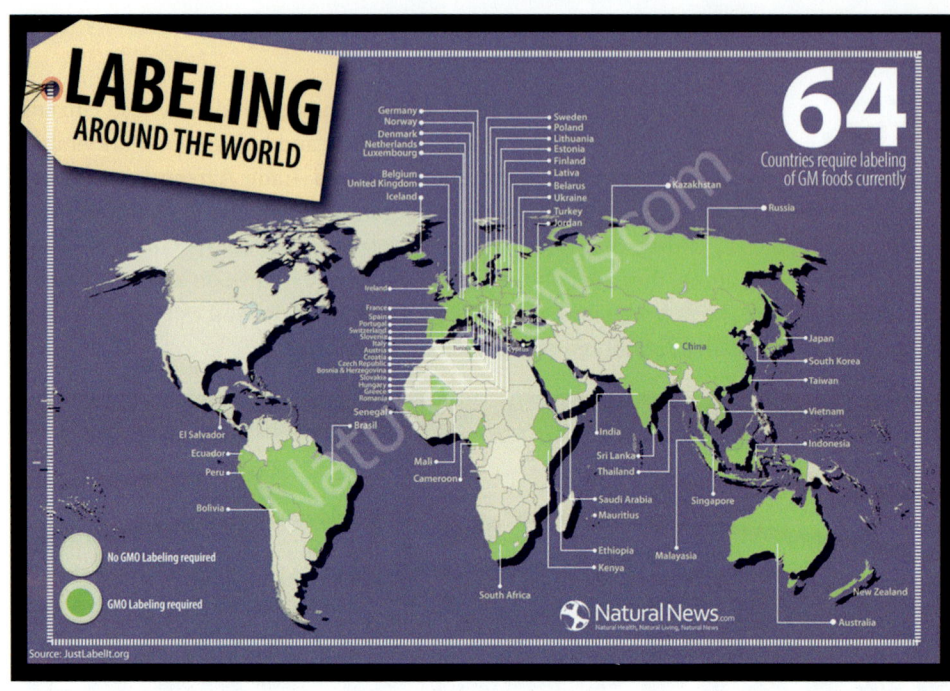

dabei vor allem große Konzerne, zum Nachteil aller. Aber: Wir können TTIP und CETA noch verhindern. Dafür brauchen wir dringend Ihre Hilfe: Bitte unterzeichnen Sie umseitig unsere selbstorganisierte Europäische Bürgerinitiative!

Sonderklagerechte* für Konzerne

Die Abkommen räumen Konzernen das Recht ein*, Staaten vor privaten Schiedsgerich-   10
ten* zu verklagen*. Das nennt sich ISDS* (Investor-Staat-Schiedsgerichtverfahren). Damit können die Konzerne gegen Gesetze oder Maßnahmen vorgehen*, durch die sie ihre Investitionen und Gewinne beeinträchtigt* sehen. Oft dienen solche Gesetze aber dem Gesundheits-, Verbraucher- und Umweltschutz.

In vielen bereits abgeschlossenen Fällen wurden Staaten zu Strafzahlungen* in Millio-   15
nen- oder sogar Milliardenhöhe verurteilt, eine Höchstgrenze existiert nicht. Die Kosten tragen die Steuerzahler/innen.

Die Klagen werden unter Ausschluss der Öffentlichkeit* vor privaten Schiedsgerichten verhandelt. Berufungsmöglichkeiten* gibt es nicht.

Erfahrungen mit bereits existierenden ISDS-Verträgen zeigen, dass sich Parlamente aus   20
Angst vor solchen Verfahren selbst beschränken, wenn es darum geht, Gesetze zum Schutz von Menschen und Umwelt zu verabschieden.

Noch mehr Macht für Konzernlobbys

Konzerne sollen möglichst frühzeitig bei Gesetzen mitreden dürfen, noch bevor Entwürfe veröffentlicht sind. Das nennen die Verhandlungsparteien beschönigend* „Regulato-   25
rische Kooperation". Sie soll den Abbau* von sozialen und ökologischen Standards zur Daueraufgabe der EU und den USA machen*.

Abbau von Verbraucherschutz

Bei einer gegenseitigen Anerkennung* von Standards gelten faktisch nur noch die jeweils schwächsten Regelungen. US-amerikanische Unternehmen könnten beispielswei-   30
se Genmais nach Europa liefern, EU-Finanzdienstleister* hochriskante Geldanlagen in den USA verkaufen.

Mit CETA und TTIP soll der europäische Markt für Kraftstoffe aus Fracking und Teersanden geöffnet werden – mit gravierenden Folgen für Umwelt und Klima.

Sonderklagerechte special rights of action
einräumen to grant
Schiedsgericht arbitral tribunal
verklagen to bring before a tribunal or court
ISDS Investor-State Dispute Settlement
vorgehen (gegen) to take legal action (against)
beeinträchtigen to affect adversely
Strafzahlung financial penalty
unter Ausschluss der Öffentlichkeit with the public excluded
Berufungsmöglichkeit possibility of appeal
beschönigend euphemistically
Abbau reduction, cutback
zur Daueraufgabe machen to make something an ongoing mission
Anerkennung recognition

Finanzdienstleister financial service provider

35 **Profite aus öffentlichen Diensten**

Liberalisierung und Privatisierung sollen zur Einbahnstraße werden. Einmal privatisierte Stadtwerke*, Krankenhäuser oder Entsorgungsfirmen* wieder in kommunale Hände zu geben, würde mit CETA und TTIP erschwert oder gar unmöglich.

Öffentliche Aufträge würden noch weiter einer Markt- und Wettbewerbslogik unterwor-
40 fen*. Lokale Wirtschaftsförderung oder sozial-ökologische Beschaffung* würde erschwert oder zum Teil verboten.

Staatliche Kulturförderung oder die Buchpreisbindung* sind in Gefahr, als Handelshemmnis* oder unerlaubte Bevorzugung* deklariert und abgeschafft zu werden.

Bürger/innen und Parlamente bleiben außen vor

45 Die Verhandlungen führt allein die EU-Kommission – im Geheimen. Sie hat bisher weder Verhandlungsmandat* noch Verhandlungstexte veröffentlicht. Das EU-Parlament stimmt am Ende nur über den fertigen Vertragstext ab, ändern kann es nichts mehr. Gleiches gilt für die nationalen Parlamente.

Üblicherweise gelten Investitionsschutzverträge* 20 Jahre und länger – damit sind sie
50 künftigen Parlamentsbeschlüssen und Volksentscheiden* nicht mehr zugänglich.

"Stop TTIP & CETA", www.stop-ttip.org [31.05.2015]

Stadtwerke public utility companies
Entsorgungsfirma waste management company
unterwerfen to be subject (to)
Beschaffung acquisition
Buchpreisbindung fixed book price/s
Handelshemmnis obstacle to trade
unerlaubte Bevorzugung illegal preference
Verhandlungsmandat negotiation mandate
Investitionsschutzvertrag investment protection agreement
Volksentscheid referendum

M 11 Genetically Engineered Animals

1. Watch a video on *YouTube* (see Webcode) in which Dr Alison Van Eenennaam, animal genomics and biotechnology specialist in the Department of Animal Science at the University of California, is interviewed on genetically engineered animals. Take notes of the scientist's explanations while watching the interview. As she talks rather fast, you may want to cast the occasional glance on the transcript. However, many of her statements will seem familiar to you.

GE Atlantic salmon that grows twice as large and twice as fast as regular salmon

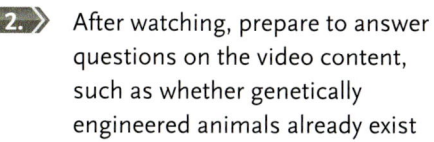

GE pig that absorbs more phytic acid (*Phytinsäure*), which in turn reduces the amount of phosphorus waste produced by the pig

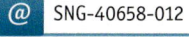
SNG-40658-012

2. After watching, prepare to answer questions on the video content, such as whether genetically engineered animals already exist and if so, why they have not yet come to market or if they ever will, or whether labelling GE foods and animal feeds should be mandatory in the U.S.

3. On one occasion, Van Eenennaam makes use of the expression "asking the crystal ball". **Explain** the stylistic device and its meaning in this context.

4. Finally, revise what you have found out in this chapter about phenomena that could pose risks for our planet and us. Which of them has the greatest risk potential in your opinion? **Justify** your conclusion.

SPEAKING TEST

A speaking test as a substitute for a written exam will usually consist of two parts and you will probably take the test in pairs or in groups of three.

Part I

In Part I you must show that you can speak about a text or a visual for about ten minutes. You will be given a preparation time of thirty minutes to work on three tasks. These tasks cover the same skills as in a written test, so there will be (1) a comprehension task, (2) an analysis task, and (3) an evaluation task.

TIPS	
Take notes only. You are required to speak freely and to establish eye contact with the interlocutors.	√
Watch your time management. You must sufficiently deal with all three tasks within ten minutes.	√
Pay attention to the task instructions. Make sure you cover all aspects of the tasks.	√
The same rules apply as in a written test. So use your own words and neutral language only in task one, apply the TEE-technique (cf. p. 115) in task two, and give a balanced assessment with reference to the text in task three.	√
Your register must be formal.	√
Guide your listeners through your talk. State what you are about to do and sum up your main results at the end of each task. Make use of varied sentence connectives.	√
Speak slowly and clearly.	√

M 12a How One Form of Chaos Breeds Another

This abridged editorial from *The Guardian*, a British centre-left national daily newspaper and winner of the Pulitzer Prize in 2014, was published on 9 March 2015.

1. **Outline** the forms of chaos that the headline refers to.

2. **Examine** the tone of the text and **explain** the purpose the editorial staff wants to achieve.

3. "As temperatures soar and southern Europe dries up, people could one day [...] move north to seek sustenance and water. We really are all in this together." (ll. 30–32). Are we really all in this together? **Comment.**

In 2014, around 3,500 boat people died trying to cross the Mediterranean to enter Europe. They risked their lives and lost. According to the UN High Commissioner for Refugees, around 218,000 people got to Europe "by irregular means" last year. They took a chance and survived.

5 Among them were those fleeing the violence in Syria, and of these, a proportion must be counted as climate refugees. Possibly because of global warming, [...] agriculture collapsed in the Fertile Crescent*, and around 1.5 million people abandoned failing farms in the countryside for Damascus and other cities. That is, they became climate refugees. Livestock was obliterated*, cereal prices doubled, and children started to sicken with nu-
10 trition-related illnesses. The 2011 Syrian uprising against the Assad regime began in the crowded settlements of climate refugees.

That label is a new one, but the idea is not just old, but prehistoric. [...] What is new is that, this time, the problem is of human making. Families are being driven from their land and livelihoods by changes effectively engineered by human action: the profligate burning
15 within the last two centuries, of fossil fuels buried in the 60m years of the carboniferous* period. [...]

In 2010 alone, 150 million were affected by floods. Flood refugees get the chance to go home when the waters recede. But in the decades to come, as rainfall patterns shift and the seas rise, some people – in Bangladesh, in Florida, in the Nile delta – will see their
20 homes submerged* forever. Islanders will find their coral atolls untenable*. California is now in the grip of catastrophic drought linked to climate change [...]. If California's vineyards and orchards* continue to desiccate*, then some could start to consider the return journey, for the same reason that Syrian and Libyan families take to the perilous* seas: because there is no choice.
25 There are many reasons for civil war and social conflict, but extremes of temperature and drought often seem to be at play. The message from the packed, unseaworthy* boats bobbing* on the Mediterranean is that people are prepared to die to get to Europe, and Europeans are not prepared to kill to stop them. There is more to come. If the climate modellers are correct, then in a few decades, the climate refugees won't only be outsiders, trying
30 to get in. As temperatures soar* and southern Europe dries up, people could one day start to abandon their farms and move north to seek sustenance* and water. We really are all in this together.

Editorial, "How One Form of Chaos Breeds Another", www.theguardian.com, 08.03.2015 [31.05.2015]

Fertile Crescent ['krɛsənt] a geographical area of fertile land in the Middle East stretching in a broad semicircle from the Nile to the Tigris and the Euphrates
to obliterate to wipe out completely

carboniferous [ˌkɑːbə'nɪfərəs] from 345 million to 280 million years ago

to submerge to disappear under water
untenable not capable of being lived in
orchard ['ɔːtʃəd] an area of land devoted to the cultivation of fruit trees
to desiccate to dry out thoroughly
perilous dangerous or risky
unseaworthy unfit for a voyage
to bob to move up and down
to soar to rise high above the normal level
sustenance ['sʌstənəns] means of livelihood

Part II

Part II will usually be a collaborative task. You will work with your partner/s on a topic that asks you to keep up a conversation. You should also be prepared to respond to questions asked by the interlocutor. Thus, in this part of the test, the focus will lie on the communicative competence needed to successfully participate in discussions. Part II is of roughly the same length as Part I.

TIPS	
Do not speak for too long, but give your partner a chance to contribute to the discussion.	√
Make sure the discussion does not get stuck. You could, for example, ask for your partner's ideas or whether he/she agrees with you or not.	√
When your partner is speaking, show that you are listening by reacting and responding appropriately. You could, for example, nod or smile as well as speak. If there is something you do not understand, ask for clarification.	√

TIPS	
Watch your time management. You must deal with both tasks and you must reach a conclusion. There will also be further questions from the interlocutor.	√
Make use of varied phrases for expressing your opinion instead of repeating "I think". Otherwise, the same language rules apply as in Part I.	√

M 12b Climate Refugees

Climate Refugees (released in the U.S. in 2010) is a multi-award winning documentary film by Michael Nash, investigating mass migration caused by our changing climate. In the following, you will find some stills from the film's trailer.

1. ➤ Take turns with your partner/s: describe the stills and make an educated guess why these scenes are shown in the documentary.

2. ➤ Together, come to a conclusion: define what exactly a climate refugee is and, against the backdrop of work done in class, name other factors that may turn people into refugees.

Megafon megaphone
Blauhelm UN soldier
gepanzertes Fahrzeug armoured vehicle
Konvoi convoy
Marsch trek
behelfsmäßiges Lager makeshift camp
ohne Dach über dem Kopf without shelter
Plastikkanister plastic canister
Erdrutsch landslide
Uferböschung embankment
verrostet rusted
Schlepperbande a gang of human traffickers
in Schach halten to keep at bay

Building a Global Mindset: The Globalization of the Individual

M1 National or Global Identity?

In a multimedia project, people of various cultural backgrounds currently living in London have been interviewed about their own values in life, their traditions, points of view and identity.

1 Ayub, England

2 Camille, Belgium

3 Shoury, India

4 Li Jing, China

5 Amy, USA

6 Mario, Mexico

7 Tadashi, Nigeria

8 Nada, Egypt

1. Select two of the interviewees and watch their interviews (Webcode → Project → Video Interviews → then click on their photographs).

2. Listen again to "your" interviewees, this time with special emphasis on their statements about national and global identity. Make notes on the relevant statements while listening.

3. **Compare** their statements about national and global identity. Where do the two think alike, where do they differ?

4. On a poster or transparency, prepare to present your findings in class.

SNG-40658-013

M2 How to Embrace Your Global Identity

Tayo Rockson

1. Revisit the "Getting started"-pages (pp. 6/7) inviting you to ask yourself whether you are a global citizen. Recall your personal answer and the criteria that led you to reach that conclusion.

2. ⟩ With reference to the writer of this blog, **state** what a TCK is.

3. ⟩ **Present** the blogger's suggestions on how to build a global mindset.

4. ⟩ **Explain** how far Rockson's suggestions are motivated by his life story.

5. ⟩ **Discuss** his mission statement, i.e. to use your difference to make a difference and embrace your global identity. Also **state** whether you would set your emphasis on the same priorities.

I made a decision earlier this year to embrace my global identity and start using it to my advantage. I'm a Third Culture Kid or TCK – someone who spent his formative* years outside of his parents' culture so I identify with many cultures (Nigerian, American and British). Some of the most common types of TCKs are missionary kids, army brats*, expats*, world travelers and diplomatic kids. I happen to fall into the diplomatic kid demographic* within the TCK community.   5

I'll use myself as an example to illustrate the different cultures I connect with. I sound mostly American even though I am completely Nigerian and I wake up early on Saturdays and Sundays to make sure I watch my favorite English Premiership team Manchester United play before Skyping with friends in England or somewhere in Europe or Africa to   10 talk about the results of the game I just watched while simultaneously thinking of the best rosters* for Fantasy Football because after all it is the most popular sport in the country I live in now.

Growing up the way I did, it became increasingly clear to me that the diversity in the world is never ending and my passion to learn more about the world has only grown so I   15 developed the following mission statement. *"Use YOUR difference to make a DIFFERENCE."*

Too many of the world's problems are a result of people being afraid of change or not being willing to understand people around them so as we get ready to wrap up* 2014, I came up with 14 things one can do to understand the world around us or use our differences to   20 make a difference. Essentially different ways to embrace *your* global identity.

Travel, Travel, Travel. You knew I was going to start with this, right? There are many ways you can travel today. For instance, you could go backpacking with friends, sign up for a tour on EF Tours* or go to a country you know nothing about and get lost! You'll learn more about people of the world by going to environments you are not familiar with.   25

Learn how to use Social Media to network. Selfies and #iwokeuplikethis are only cool for about 15 minutes before the next greatest selfie hits the scene. So instead of focusing on 15 minutes of social media fame, try connecting with other people. Use those hashtags to start conversations. For example, before I launched my podcast, I spent weeks connecting with other Third Culture Kids by typing the #ThirdCultureKid and #TCK into the search   30 bar on Twitter and inserting myself in conversations happening around these hash tags. As a result of this, I made some really cool new friends that live all over. Find a couple of hashtags that align* with your passions and go network. Who knows maybe you'll be taking group shots with your new friends as you're launching your newest company or celebrating a victory in your intramural* sports league instead of taking your 20th selfie. I   35 should say that I have nothing against selfies but there needs to be a healthy balance of "I" and "we" in today's world. Social Media shouldn't just be a way to keep in touch with friends and family, it can also be a great way to raise awareness about social issues or even raise money for a cause. You could start a Facebook group that educates your friends about an issue that you are passionate about or use that page to tell family and friends why   40 their money will help you achieve whatever goal you want to achieve.

---

formative relating to formation, development, or growth
army brat a child of a career military
expat a person who is voluntarily absent from home or country
demographic a portion of the population

roster a list of the names of players on a sports team

to wrap up *here:* to bring something to an end

EF Tours (EF =Education First) an international education company that specialises in language training, educational travel, academic degree programs, and cultural exchange

to align [əˈlaɪn] to match

intramural carried on within the walls of an institution or school

Speaking of intramural sports join a sports league. Sports forms bonds across cultures like no other. You learn a lot about people and how to work together as a team. Both of which are great ways to learn how to connect with people.

45 **More History, Travel and National Geographic. Less Reality TV.** Pretty self-explanatory. They often say people who forget history are bound to repeat it and I see this every day. I hear so many ignorant statements every day and it is because people aren't watching the right things. Spend about 30 minutes to 2 hours a day on any or all of these channels I mentioned above and watch as your mind expands*. Reading/watching National Geo-
50 graphic can also help make you a better environmental citizen. You can learn about differ- ent ways to help your environment and animals.

Volunteer anywhere. Helping others can allow you to learn about other people's stories and stories are a great way to learn about other people.

Mentor someone. A few things can happen here. You teach another individual how to be
55 a better citizen of their community, you can help someone become better at a skill, and you can become a better person by making someone better. Too many "betters" for you not to be doing this right now. By sharing your skill-set with someone else, you are giving your unique self to the world and helping to break the homogenous* cycle many people get stuck in.

60 **Be untraditional.** I am allergic to homogenous. In fact, I just sneezed now thinking of it. It's time to break what I call the "supposed to syndrome". That mindset stifles* innova- tion and doesn't allow us to make maximum impact or embrace other cultures. It's not a bad thing to look different from someone or speak another language. It's a beautiful thing so strive* to be different and apply other cultures into your everyday life.

65 **Speaking of language, learn a new one.** Can you imagine the new set of people you can talk to and potentially influence just by speaking another language?

Read wide and far. I talked earlier about having more National Geographic, Travel and History channel in your life. Add books also to that equation*. Read everything from the classics to the *Hunger Games*. Everything from nonfiction to fiction. There is no telling
70 what knowledge about the world you can gain just by reading different people's perspec- tives manifested through protagonists and antagonists.

Read *The Alchemist**. I'm not done with books just yet. This is probably one of my favorite books of all time. It details the different lessons that young Santiago learns about the world and himself while traveling and seeking his personal legend. You'll see some of the
75 amazing things you can discover by understanding the world.

Go to conferences. Going to conferences that are dedicated to your passion can help turn you into difference makers because you get to hear from likeminded people who could be potential mentors or certain speeches can spark* an idea in your head. Earlier this year, I went to a two-day event for Arianna Huffington's book* and she made a casual statement
80 about how her kids used to joke about her accent and the idea for my first eBook was sparked and I immediately rebranded* my website to what it is now. It occurred to me that there were many people out there like Arianna and me who don't look like how they are supposed to sound or sound like how they are supposed to look and I got to work. Communities, masterminds, and difference making friendships are formed at confer-
85 ences. Go to at least two a year.

Start a blog. I believe in using media for good and not allowing media to use us. One way to do this is to start a blog and share your opinion on something. Who knows, maybe you'll gain a following and make some more friends. People connect with stories and are influenced by the fact that they are not the only ones going through something where it's
90 good or bad.

to expand to open up

homogenous [hə'mɒdʒɪnəs] all of the same kind or nature

to stifle to cut off or repress

to strive to make a great effort

equation *Gleichung*

The Alchemist novel by Paulo Coelho (1988)

to spark to set in motion
Arianna Huffington's book *On Becoming Fearless … in Love, Work, and Life (2007)*
to rebrand to update the image of

Start a podcast. Speaking of using media for good. Why not podcast. It's essentially radio on demand and you can do it anywhere in the world.

Invest In Yourself. You can't be a difference maker if you don't put in the time to educate and develop yourself.

As I often say, I want to bring East and West together and have them sit side by side with North and South to trade stories of adventures and experiences they each have had. Now go forth and be world changers! *Use your DIFFERENCE to make a DIFFERENCE.*

Tayo Rockson, "14 Ways to Embrace Your Global Identity", www.huffingtonpost.com, 30.09.2014 [31.05.2015], with contributions from Tayo Rockson, Founder of UYD Media (www.uydmedia.com)

M3 Global Citizen Internships

1. ≫ **Outline** AIESEC's Global Citizen programme, as presented in the advertisement.

2. ≫ **State** the reasons they give for becoming a global citizen.

3. ≫ Which of the four areas offered would you personally be interested in? **Justify** your choice.

4. ≫ Imagine you qualify for a Global Citizen internship, i. e. you are at least 18 years old and are currently studying at a University or University of Applied Sciences. Write the letter of motivation accompanying your CV (curriculum vitae, *Lebenslauf*) for your internship application with AIESEC (cf. skills box).

The Global Citizen programme enables young people to directly impact communities abroad through volunteer internships, as well as develop themselves personally and professionally by gaining practical skills and by experiencing a new culture.

Global Citizen internships are typically 6–8 weeks and allow youth to make a positive impact in society in the areas of Cultural Understanding, Literacy*, Social Entrepreneurship and the Environment.

literacy [ˈlɪtərəsi] (1) the ability to read and write; (2) the ability to use language proficiently

to showcase to exhibit or display

Develop activities and events to showcase* your culture and promote cross-cultural understanding in communities abroad. Become a Global Citizen by being an ambassador* of your country and learning about the culture of your host country.

ambassador *here:* an unofficial representative

Empower a nation's next generation of leaders. Provide children, teenagers, and young adults with access to basic education through language education, skills development and youth empowerment.

Gain practical experience by applying business knowledge to address issues faced by NGOs* and small businesses around the world. Work on marketing and fundraising strategies, and educate young people on entrepreneurship skills.

Create and promote projects dealing with sustainable development and promote environmental awareness on topics such as energy conservation, pollution and climate change.

NGO non-governmental organisation

Why Global Citizen?
Challenge Yourself
Experience intense personal and professional development on a Global Talent internship. Acquire real-world leadership skills such as communication, critical thinking and adapt-ability* in a challenging cultural environment.
Think Globally
The Canadian Chamber of Commerce ranks lack of globalization as one of the top barriers to Canadian competitiveness. By developing a better understanding of our globalized world, you will be ahead of the game* and valued by employers.
Impact Society
Contribute to a company abroad through a Global Talent internship to directly improve the lives of the community.
Want to work abroad?
Then apply for an internship with AIESEC, Canada.

AIESEC, whose name comes from the French acronym for *Association internationale des étudiants en sciences économiques et commerciales*, was founded in Europe in 1948. The organisation's headquarters is in Rotterdam, Holland, and additionally, there are more than 100 national offices around the world, including the one in Toronto, Canada.
AIESEC, "Global Citizen", http://aiesec.ca [16.05.15]

10

adaptability the ability to change (or be changed) to fit changed circumstances

15

to be ahead of the game (*coll.*) to know more about the most recent developments in a particular subject or activity than the people (or companies) with whom you are competing, *einen Schritt voraus sein*

20

Zoom in: Skills

Writing a letter of motivation
A letter of motivation is a one-page document that introduces your CV.
Outline:
Your full address, city, zip code (*align all text left*)
Date
Name and title of the specific person to address the letter to
(*call ahead to ask who is responsible*)
Organisation name
Full address

Dear Mr/Ms ...., *(continue with a capital letter – despite the comma!)*
The first paragraph should introduce: (1) the internship you are applying for and (2) how you heard about it.
The second/main paragraph should include: (3) two or three skills that make you particularly suited for the internship in the area of your choice, and (4) an explanation of how you have developed each skill through past experiences.
The third paragraph should conclude with: (5) re-stating why you will be an asset to the organisation, (6) expressing your wish for an interview, and (7) thanking them for their time and consideration.
Sincerely,
Your signature followed by your full name typed

5. Search the web to find internship, voluntary social year or similar programmes abroad that you could apply for right after passing your entrance qualification for studying at a University or University of Applied Sciences. Together, compile a dossier ['dɒsieɪ] containing all the available data and discuss them in class.

M 4   English as the *Lingua Franca*

Although there are differences between English-speaking countries, the United Kingdom, the United States, Canada, Australia, and New Zealand share common characteristics. In the majority of countries, among them the European countries (and in particular Scandinavia), or India and Brazil, to name but a few examples, English has meanwhile become the *lingua franca*, i.e. the language used between groups of people who speak different languages. Subsequently, if you are going abroad to work or study, you should be familiar with globally understood descriptions of language proficiency (competence).

1. The following terms, starting with the highest level of proficiency, are commonly used in job, internship or college placement applications written in English: native speaker – near native/fluent – excellent command/highly proficient in spoken and written English – very good command – good command – basic communication skills. Think about what level of language proficiency you would place yourself on.

2. **Summarise** the proficiency levels of the CEF, differentiating them from one another.

3. **Explain** the use of a framework such as the CEF, published in 2001 and now available in 38 languages.

4. "The Framework [...] must not be treated as sacred (or indeed nefarious*!). It is an instrument of reference, not an object of reverence*. The six levels must not be confused with the Ten Commandments*." (Daniel Coste, *Contextualising Uses of the Common European Framework of Reference for Languages*, Council of Europe, Strasbourg 2007). **Comment** on Coste's assertion.

nefarious evil or sinful
reverence ['rɛvərəns] a feeling or attitude of profound respect
Ten Commandments (*Old Testament*) the commandments summarising the basic obligations of man towards God and his fellow men, delivered to Moses on Mount Sinai engraved on two tables of stone (*Exodus 20,1–17*)

The Council of Europe has introduced the Common European Framework of Reference for Languages (CEF) to provide a comprehensive and transparent system for describing levels of language proficiency and for the easy comparison of language qualifications. The

CEF is now widely used as a standard by educational establishments, language testing
systems and publishers of language-learning materials throughout Europe.

The system describes what a learner should be able to do in listening, speaking, reading
and writing at six levels of language proficiency as follows:

Proficient user   C2 Mastery

Can understand with ease virtually everything heard or read. Can summarise information
from different spoken and written sources, reconstructing arguments and accounts in a
coherent presentation. Can express him/herself spontaneously, very fluently and pre-
cisely, differentiating finer shades of meaning even in more complex situations.

C1 Effective Operational* Proficiency

Can understand a wide range of demanding, longer texts, and recognise implicit* meaning. Can express him/herself fluently and spontaneously without much obvious searching
for expressions. Can use language flexibly and effectively for social, academic and professional purposes. Can produce clear, well-structured, detailed text on complex subjects,
showing controlled use of organisational patterns, connectors and cohesive* devices.

Independent user   B2 Vantage*

Can understand the main ideas of complex text on both concrete and abstract topics, including technical discussions in his/her field of specialisation. Can interact with a degree
of fluency and spontaneity that makes regular interaction with native speakers quite possible without strain* for either party. Can produce clear, detailed text on a wide range of
subjects and explain a viewpoint on a topical issue giving the advantages and disadvantages of various options.

B1 Threshold*

Can understand the main points of clear standard input on familiar matters regularly
encountered in work, school, leisure, etc. Can deal with most situations likely to arise
whilst travelling in an area where the language is spoken. Can produce simple connected
text on topics which are familiar or of personal interest. Can describe experiences and
events, dreams, hopes & ambitions and briefly give reasons and explanations for opinions
and plans.

Basic user   A2 Waystage*

Can understand sentences and frequently used expressions related to areas of most immediate relevance (e. g. very basic personal and family information, shopping, local geography, employment). Can communicate in simple and routine tasks requiring a simple
and direct exchange of information on familiar and routine matters. Can describe in
simple terms aspects of his/her background, immediate environment and matters in areas of immediate need.

A1 Breakthrough

Can understand and use familiar everyday expressions and very basic phrases aimed at
the satisfaction of needs of a concrete type. Can introduce him/herself and others and can
ask and answer questions about personal details such as where he/she lives, people he/
she knows and things he/she has. Can interact in a simple way provided the other person
talks slowly and clearly and is prepared to help.

The CEF enables you to give differentiated descriptions of your individual language skills.
You can say, for example, that your level of proficiency in writing English is B2, whereas
your spoken English is C1. The CEF also helps you to give a very detailed description of
your language skills if you are applying for a job for which languages are a key aspect of
the job.

---

operational ready for use
implicit implied though
not directly expressed

cohesive joining bits and
pieces into a unified
whole
vantage superiority

strain stress

threshold the starting
point of an experience or
venture, *Schwelle*

waystage a low to middle
level of ability in a foreign
language

If you are applying for a job or scholarship in English within Europe, you can add the CEF level in brackets if you think it will be understood. For example: English: highly proficient in both spoken and written English (Common European Framework C1).

Ludwig-Maximilians-Universität München, "Describing Language Skills", www.jobline.uni-muenchen.de [31.05.2015]

M 5 Global Reading Challenge

Tayo Rockson recommended, among other things, reading "far and wide" to be able to understand the world and develop a global mindset (cf. M 2). So what about expanding your horizon by arranging a global reading challenge in class? Ask your English teacher if he/she could hand out a list of novels for young adults from different continents that allow for a focus on the experience of social and cultural difference and diversity. Select one of the books, read it at home within the period agreed, then present 'your' global novel to the class. When preparing your presentation, ask yourself the following questions:

1. ⟩⟩ What is this narrative about? What surprised you about the setting and characters? What are the evident issues concerning cultural difference and diversity in this text?

2. ⟩⟩ Who wrote this book, and from what perspective? Who is the readership? How does the text work to support or challenge the ways of understanding oneself and others in the world?

3. ⟩⟩ What are the implications of the text for local adolescents or young adults? What critical actions might they be led to take in the light of their reading?

Here are some suggestions for global-novel reading to get you started.

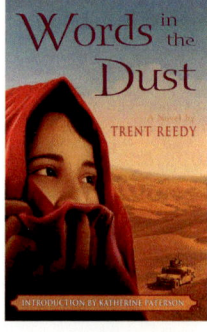

Trent Reedy, *Words in the Dust*, Arthur A. Levine Books, New York 2013 – Afghanistan

Born with a cleft lip. Zulaikha struggles to feel worth in a society that values women by their marriage prospects: "What bride-price would Baba get for me? Maybe one Afghani?" Then, by chance, Zulaikha meets Meena, a former professor, who begins to teach her to read and write just as American soldiers arrive, bringing the chance for both more education and surgery to correct Zulaikha's birth defect. Reedy based his debut on real people and places he encountered while serving with the National Guard in Afghanistan.

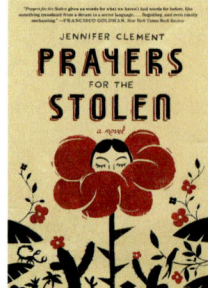

Jennifer Clement, *Prayers for the Stolen*, Random House, London 2014 – Mexico

The setting is Guerrero, Mexico, known for mass murders, mass kidnappings and deep-rooted government corruption. The characters are surrounded by gang violence and especially the human trafficking of women and girls. In a poor mountain village with no fathers or husbands for protection, where calling the police equals inviting trouble, the girls have to make themselves appear boyish and ugly, in order to avoid being stolen.

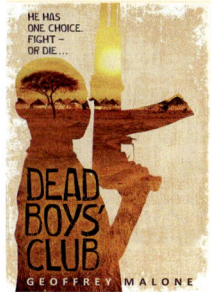

Geoffrey Malone, *Dead Boys Club*,
Hachette Children's Group, London 2013 – Uganda

'If they ever come here,' his father had warned, 'drop everything. Just run and hide!' And now they were here. God's Freedom Army. Bringers of blood and suffering. Rebels! Killers! Everyone of them. Hundreds of thousands of children are abducted from their homes and used as boy soldiers. This is the story of one of them. 12-year-old Sam is ripped from his village in Uganda and forced to march with rebel soldiers to their training camp in southern Sudan.

Texts taken from: www.amazon.de [31.05.2015]

 4. When applying the finishing touches to your presentation, make a self-assessment by means of the questions in the flow chart. If you can answer them positively, you have every reason to proudly present your work to your classmates.

procrastination putting off or deferring an action to a later time

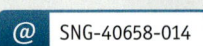

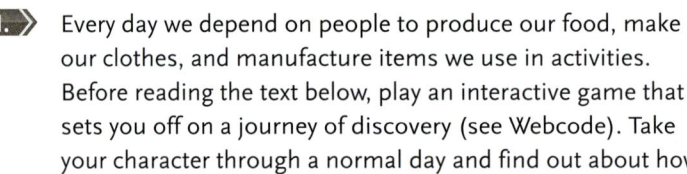

M 6   Fair Trade

Chris Woodford

1. ➤ Every day we depend on people to produce our food, make our clothes, and manufacture items we use in activities. Before reading the text below, play an interactive game that sets you off on a journey of discovery (see Webcode). Take your character through a normal day and find out about how many different countries you rely on.

2. ➤ Now read the first text excerpt thoroughly, underline the questions that subdivide the text as well as the key words and phrases that answer them. Visualise the text structure (cf. skills pages).

3. ➤ Based on your visualisation, **summarise** the text.

4. ➤ **Examine** the language Woodford uses to explain to us the meaning of 'fair trade' as opposed to 'unfair trade'.

5. ➤ Finally, read the second text excerpt. Then, against the backdrop of the examples given in this excerpt, **evaluate** whether Woodford is right in saying that "out of sight [is] out of mind" (l. 85).

Excerpt 1

Bargain ... or exploitation?

Everyone likes a bargain, but you have to wonder about a T-shirt that costs only five dollars. How is it possible for someone to grow the cotton, harvest it, make it into a shirt, transport it, sell it on to a retailer*, and still make a profit for a price like that? The answer should be blindingly obvious, but we choose to ignore it. Cut-price clothes and food are all ⁵ too often produced by exploiting people in developing countries, who make the cheap goods we've come to love by working long hours for low pay, often in appalling* conditions. We try not to put up with this in our countries, but when the label says "Made in India" or "Made in Chile", we conveniently push it to the back of our minds. Fortunately, many people are waking up to the basic unfairness of world trade and demanding a better ¹⁰ deal for the people who do our dirty work. It's called fair trade. Let's find out why it's important and how it works. [...]

Why does free trade often mean unfair trade?

Globalization – the tendency of companies to treat the world as one giant kingdom of potential profit, without all those pesky* borders – is largely to blame. If a company can ¹⁵ sew its jeans in Honduras for a fraction the price it can do it in Chicago, the decision to outsource is a no-brainer*. [...]

Free trade is a part of globalization and it sounds great in theory: if we removed all barriers to trade, such as import tariffs (the taxes companies have to pay to get their goods into another country and sell them there), all countries could compete on a level* playing field ²⁰ – and what could be fairer than that? In practice, it doesn't work out quite like that. Some countries are inevitably far more powerful than others and they want things to stay that way. Even while promoting free trade, they use all kinds of tactics to ensure they can trade more freely than other people. You might have heard of a practice called dumping? That's where an industrialized country subsidizes* the production of finished goods, which it ²⁵ then exports to a developing country at a price that's lower than the goods the developing

---

retailer a merchant who sells goods in small quantities directly to consumers
appalling [əˈpɔːlɪŋ] causing horror or disgust

pesky troublesome, annoying

a no-brainer something that requires little or no mental effort

level (adj.) even

to subsidize to give financial aid

country can produce at home. The developing country has to cut the prices of its own goods to a level that makes it impossible for poorer people to support themselves. Another tactic is for rich countries to impose high tariffs on finished goods but low tariffs on basic, raw materials. That gives poorer countries no option but to export raw materials: they can't turn those materials into high-value finished goods themselves because they won't be able to

Fair trade coffee, tea and sugar

export them. The rich countries import the low-value, raw materials, make them into high-value finished goods wherever it suits them, then export the finished goods back to the poor countries. Practices like this mean free trade is all too often a synonym for unfair trade. [...]

What is fair trade?

Fair trade is a different system that starts from the premise that workers' lives have a value; this social benefit is partly what you pay for when you buy something. Fair trade doesn't just mean farmers and producers receive more money so they can support their families in the short term – though that's vitally important. It also means they work under long-term contracts so their communities have enough security to invest in improvements both to their businesses (with more land or animals or better machinery) and their societies (with things like schools or health clinics). Typically, fair-trade producers are small cooperatives of workers using no child or forced labor, using organic or environmentally sustainable methods, and having high standards of animal welfare. Workers are free to join unions and bargain collectively to help improve their lives. Typically, fair trade producers sign up to some sort of labelling scheme that guarantees things have been made under good conditions. [...]

Achieving truly fair trade means seeing the world in a different way, as a planet of partnership and mutual prosperity rather than plunder and exploitation. Fair trade is not about paying 50 cents more for your coffee; it's about caring for your "neighbors" – even when they're on the other side of the world.

Excerpt 2

It's easy to find cheap goods on Main Street, but finding out why they cost so little isn't always so easy:

- How about that cotton T-shirt you just bought for $5? Oxfam tells us: "A typical cotton producing household in West Africa has about 10 family members, an average life expectancy of about 48 years and an adult literacy rate of less than 25 percent. Cotton is often the only source of cash income for these families who live on less than $1 a day per person."[1]
- What about the oranges from Chile you just put in your shopping cart? Oxfam again: "In the fruit-picking sector, 75 % of women work more than 60 hours a week in season, on temporary contracts, and a third of them do not earn even the minimum wage."[2]

Brands like *No Sweat* are rejecting unfair, sweatshop labour. Unlike some footwear brands, these popular sneakers are made by trade-union members who earn a decent wage and work in good conditions.

● Maybe you fancy a nice bunch of cut flowers for your mom? Co-op America tells us that
over two thirds of American flowers are imported, typically from countries where ₇₅
cheap labor and poor regulation of toxic pesticides is commonplace: "In Ecuador, nearly 60 % of flower workers surveyed showed poisoning symptoms, including headaches,
dizziness, trembling hands and blurred vision."³ And these are some of the less extreme examples, before we even start talking about child labor and sweatshops.

Why do we put up with this kind of thing? According to Co-op America, the answer is ₈₀
obvious: "Ultimately, sweatshops* exist because the human links of the supply chain are
hidden from us when we shop. If working conditions at producer factories were visible to
consumers at the point of purchase*, it would be harder to convince shoppers that cheaper goods are worth the price of worker abuse."⁴

That's another way of saying "out of sight, out of mind". ₈₅

---

¹ Reform of US cotton subsidies could feed and educate millions in poor west African countries, Oxfam International press release, 22 June 2007 (via Wayback Machine)
² Chilean fruit-picking workers' story, Oxfam International campaign page (via Wayback Machine)
³ Fair trade: Flowers, Green America
⁴ Guide to Ending sweatshops, Green America (PDF file)
Chris Woodford, "Fair Trade", www.explainthatstuff.com, 24.09.2014 [31.05.2015], Chris Woodford/Explainthatstuff.com

M7 How Small Changes Can Have a Global Impact

Claudia Juech

1. ⟩ **Summarise** how, according to Juech, each of us can make choices that may lead to
small but distinct differences.

2. ⟩ **Analyse** the way she states her case and tries to convince her readers.

3. ⟩ Has Juech succeeded in convincing you? If so, **justify** why and **state** what change
you would like to be (cf. l. 55). If not, **explain** why not.

As individuals we sometimes feel that there is very little that we can do in the face of big
global challenges such as pandemics, financial crises or climate change. But if we dig
deeper into what's causing those problems we often find that the way we live is an important contributing factor.

This means that if large numbers of people started behaving differently, many small ₅
changes can have truly big effects (such as the introduction of hand-washing in the late
1900s as a "do-it-yourself" vaccine*). The necessity for lifestyle changes doesn't exoner-
ate* institutional actors, including governments, corporations or non-profits. They have
an important role to play in providing nudges* that entice* us to make better choices
benefiting our health, environment and finances. ₁₀

Behavioural change is tough. Information, motivation and ability need to come together
to make it happen, and to keep it up requires removing many of the obstacles that make
us fall back into old patterns – customs, convenience*, the desire for instant gratification*
to only name a few. In recent years, scientists, advertisers and designers have come up
with innovative ways to make changes easier and fun. ₁₅

Gamification* is one approach that has proven to be successful in a variety of contexts.
Wearing a seatbelt is known to reduce serious injuries and deaths by about half, yet 55 %
of teens (aged 13 – 20 years) that died in car accidents in the US in 2012 weren't wearing

their seatbelt at the time of the crash. *Play belt*,
20 an idea by Nevana Stojanovic from Serbia, is a
safety belt that only turns on the in-car entertainment system when the belt is in use. It
works because it addresses the underlying
cause of our dangerous inaction – motivation,
25 not a lack of information or ability.

In the future, many of us will have instant information about our own behaviour at our fin-
gertips. Wearable technologies will provide
feedback on our sleep patterns, physical activ-
30 ity, eating habits and much more. But will it
change our behaviour? Not necessarily. However, in combination with approaches that al-
low for peer* comparison and support, the results change dramatically.

One example from the energy sector was developed by *Opower*, a software company in the
35 utility* sector. Its report includes a grade that assesses energy consumption in relation to
others in the neighbourhood. Two smiley faces are given if the household used less than
80 % of its neighbour's consumption: one if consumption was lower than 50 %; none if
usage was higher than most neighbours. As soon as customers received their first reports
and saw the smiley face box, they began increasing their energy efficiency. This approach
40 combines a number of aspects – it speaks to our perception of our ability, gives us actionable* information and triggers* our competitive spirit. If our neighbours can save energy,
we can too.

Lastly, when it comes to making financial decisions we humans too often rely on our gut*
and immediate impulses instead of analytically considering our longer-term needs. Hu-
45 man-centred design approaches don't work with how we *should* make decisions in an
idealized world, but are grounded* in our "imperfect" reality. *Piggymojo*, for example, allows individuals to link up with their significant other or another partner and work together towards a savings goal. Instead of impulse buys, *Piggymojo* records "impulse saves"
(deciding not to buy that cup of coffee, for example), which are shared with the savings
50 partner, and tracked by the service towards your goal. [...]

These examples are only small illustrations of how each one of us can influence how we
as individuals can become more resilient* by making choices that improve our health,
protect our environment and build a financial safety net, and how simple approaches can
make that more fun and sustainable.
55 What's the change that you want to be?*

Claudia Juech, "How Small Changes Can Have a Global Impact", http://agenda.weforum.org, 19.05.2015 [31.05.15]

"IMPLEMENTING THESE CHANGES WON'T BE EASY. WE'RE PRETTY SET IN DOING THINGS THE WRONG WAY."

peer a person who has equal standing with others, as in rank, class, or age
utility/-ies water, electricity, gas

actionable that allows a decision to be made
to trigger to set off, to spark
gut (*slang*) innermost emotional response

grounded (in) based (on)

resilient able to withstand difficult conditions

"Be the change that you wish to see in the world." (Mahatma Ghandi)

M8 Viral Video* Challenges
M8a "Happy" Dances around the World

viral video a video that (spreads like a virus and) becomes popular through Internet sharing

Pharrell [fə'rɛl] Williams's song "Happy" was released in November 2013 alongside a
24-hour music video, a novel concept featuring ordinary people dancing to the bouncy
song in the streets. A version of it, which went viral on *YouTube*, marked the beginning of
an unprecedented global movement of happiness as fans from dozens of countries uploaded homemade videos to a website dedicated to Pharrell.

@ SNG-40658-015

@ SNG-40658-016

1. ▶ Watch and **describe** the initial four-minute version of the music video (see webcode).

2. ▶ **Examine** what specific elements turn "Happy" into a universal feel-good song.

3. ▶ Select two or three of almost 2,000 videos from more than 150 countries that people have uploaded to show their gratitude to Pharrell and share their happiness with you (see Webcode). Just click on a city name to watch the video of your choice. **Assess** the global impact of making your own choreographed music video and putting it online.

M 8b   The ALS "Ice Bucket Challenge"

On *Facebook, YouTube, Twitter* or other networking sites, you have probably seen videos of people pouring a bucket of ice-cold water over their heads. They have taken part in the "Ice Bucket Challenge", one of the most viral philanthropic* social media campaigns in history. The challenge involves dumping ice water on top of your head or donating $100 to various ALS (Amyotrophic Lateral Sclerosis, cf. infographic) charities. "Ice Bucket Challenge" participants post their homemade videos online and invite friends to follow suit*. In that way, more than US$115 million have been donated since 29 July 2014 for the purpose of alleviating* the suffering of people affected by this fatal disease.

philanthropic
[ˌfɪlənˈθrɒpɪk] showing concern for humanity, especially by being charitable and donating money
to follow suit to follow a person's example or imitate
to alleviate [əˈliːvieɪt] to make easier to endure, to relieve

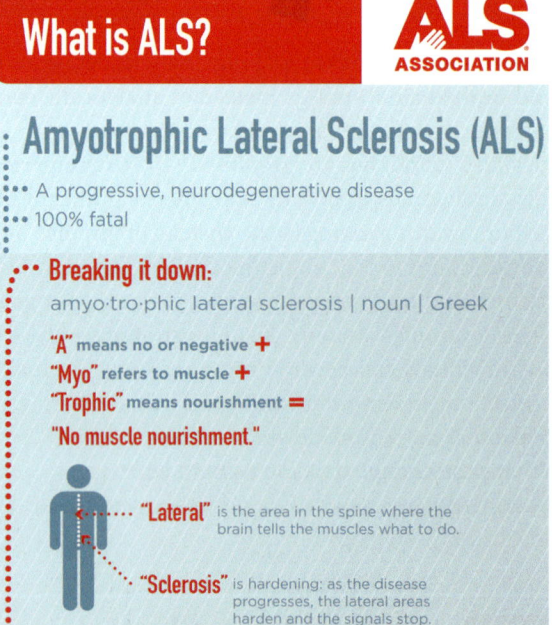

What is ALS?

ALS ASSOCIATION

Amyotrophic Lateral Sclerosis (ALS)

• • A progressive, neurodegenerative disease
• • 100% fatal

Breaking it down:
amyo·tro·phic lateral sclerosis | noun | Greek

"A" means no or negative **+**
"Myo" refers to muscle **+**
"Trophic" means nourishment **=**

"No muscle nourishment."

"Lateral" is the area in the spine where the brain tells the muscles what to do.

"Sclerosis" is hardening: as the disease progresses, the lateral areas harden and the signals stop.

1. ▶ The infographic above gives a short introduction as to what ALS is. Do further research on the disease.

@ SNG-40658-017

2. ▶ Watch and **describe** the one-minute "Ice Bucket Challenge" video of the non-profit ALS Association thanking all participants for supporting their fight against the disease (see Webcode).

3. Celebrities from former U.S. President George W. Bush to Lady Gaga have accepted the "Ice Bucket Challenge" (see Webcode). Search the net to find out whether your favourite stars have also gone along with the challenge. Share the results of your research with a partner.

4. **Compare** the two viral video challenges (M 8a and M 8b) and **point out** similarities as well as the main difference/s.

5. There have been quite a few worries concerning the motives of the people participating in the "Ice Bucket Challenge". Do these people really care about ALS, or do they just want to gain the respect of others? Or do they have other motives for presenting themselves on the Internet? **Discuss**.

ZOOM IN: People

For most people, the name **Stephen Hawking** (born in Oxford, UK, in 1942) calls to mind the brilliant, wheel chair-bound physicist and his renowned theories about space-time and black holes. However, a new film, *The Theory of Everything*, tells the story of Hawking's life and his struggle with **ALS**. In the movie, actor Eddie Redmayne (photo) portrays Hawking's physical decline as a result of the fatal disease.

Tanya Lewis, "Stephen Hawking Film Depicts Courageous Battle with Disease", www.livescience.com, 05.11.2014 [19.05.2015]

M 9 Theme Poetry Slam

Now that you have devoted your attention to the subject of globalization across four chapters, it is high time for you to cast a final glance at the aspect of building a global mindset and have some fun while doing so. Let us therefore organise a slam, delivering our personal messages on how to become a global citizen (= theme).

ZOOM IN: Skills

A **Theme Poetry Slam** is a live competition in which the participants read or recite their own poetry or prose on a specified theme. It is a spoken-word event that stimulates creativity, improves language skills and aims at entertaining the audience. The 'poetry' or 'spoken words', performed on stage to be *heard*, can be of any style as the slam format is open to all approaches to recital and performance.

Basic rules of a Poetry Slam:

- Each poem must be of the participant's own construction.
- Each participant gets three minutes to read or recite one poem.
- The participant may not use props, costumes or musical instruments.
- Five judges are selected from the audience. Of the scores the participant receives from these five judges, the high and low scores are dropped and the remaining three are averaged, giving the participant a total score of 0–30.

SNG-40658-019

Pre-slam activities

1. Watch an example of slam poetry on *YouTube* (see Webcode), e.g. (1) Belissa, Rhiannon and Zariya's slam poem "Somewhere in America", which points out that some of the greatest injustices in the U.S. are also the least-talked about, both in school textbooks and in life. The three teens are members of the *Get Lit* organisation, a non-profit group that uses the spoken word to improve literacy rates in Los Angeles.
Or (2) Taylor Mali's viral poem "What Teachers Make", asking what students can possibly learn from someone who has decided that his or her best option in life is to become a teacher. Mali is one of the best slam poets working today and has appeared many times on teams at the British National Poetry Slam.

2. Although the slam itself is a spoken-word event, you will have to get words onto paper before turning them into some sort of poem. So revise the material of this chapter to get an idea on what, in your opinion, makes a committed cosmopolitan. During this creative process, do not worry about grammar or spelling; just keep writing.

3. As your words are meant for an audience, you should ask yourself the following questions before editing your poem: have I left out everything that is superfluous to my message? Is my message clear and easy to understand? What rhetorical means can I use (rhyme, rhythm, repetition, wordplay, alliteration, imagery, etc.)? You may also ask a classmate or your teacher to check your poem for mistakes that could make comprehension difficult.

4. Learning your poem by heart will make you feel more at ease before your audience; this is, however, not an obligation. Rehearse your performance in front of a mirror or in front of your parents and/or friends. Keep in mind that you have only three minutes to recite your work, so set the alarm clock or assign the task of timekeeper to a person of your choice.

Enjoy and good luck!

Zoom in: Words in Context

Shaping the Future: Drivers of Global Change	
abundant, abundance	reichlich (vorhanden), Überfluss
adverse, adversity, adversary	widrig/schädlich, Ungemach/Widrigkeit, Widersacher/in
to advocate, advocate	befürworten/plädieren für, Verfechter/in
algorithm	Verfahren/Rechenregel
artificial intelligence	künstliche Intelligenz
to affect, effect, effective	betreffen/beeinflussen, Auswirkung, wirksam
austere, austerity	karg/genügsam, Einschränkung/Entbehrung
to benefit, benefit, beneficial	profitieren/zugutekommen, Vorteil/Nutzen, nützlich/segensreich
breach of privacy	Verletzung der Privatsphäre
bot	Roboter zum Durchsuchen von Webseiten
cataclysm	Katastrophe/(gewaltsame) Umwälzung
cloud computing	Datenspeicherung in entferntem Rechenzentrum
to commit oneself, commitment	sich engagieren, Engagement
to conglomerate, conglomerate	sich zusammenballen, Mischkonzern/(buntes) Gemisch
detriment, to be detrimental to	Nachteil, zum Nachteil gereichen
digital divide	Kluft im Zugang zu Informations- und Kommunikationstechnologie
to drive, drive, driver, driving force	antreiben, Antrieb, Motor, Triebfeder
efficacy, cost-efficient	Effizienz/Leistungsfähigkeit, kostengünstig/rentabel
to elicit information	Informationen entlocken
to emerge, emergence	entstehen/auftauchen, Aufkommen
expedient, expedient, to hit on an expedient	Hilfsmittel/Behelf/Notlösung, zweckdienlich/opportun, einen Ausweg finden
fake account	gefälschtes Benutzerkonto
inexorable, inexorability	unerbittlich, Unerbittlichkeit
intricate, to express something in an intricate way	kompliziert/komplex, etwas verklausulieren
to leak, leak	durchsickern (lassen), undichte Stelle
livelihood/sustenance	Lebensunterhalt/Existenzgrundlage
offshore company	Briefkastenfirma
onerous, onerousness	belastend/lästig, Last
onslaught, to make an onslaught on	Angriff/e, angreifen
to outsource, outsourcing	ausgliedern, Auslagerung/Fremdvergabe
repercussion	Rückwirkung/Rückschlag
robosourcing	Verlagerung von Aufgaben an automatisierte Maschinen
utility	Nutzen/Brauchbarkeit; Versorger
vicious cycle/circle	Teufelskreis
to wage war against/on; proxy war	Krieg führen; Stellvertreterkrieg

Breaking the Equilibrium: The Reality of Our Shrinking World	
to abduct, abduction	verschleppen, Verschleppung
to achieve equal pay	gleiche Entlohnung verwirklichen/zustande bringen
airborne transmission	Übertragung durch die Luft
to alienate, alienation	entfremden, Entfremdung
to assault, assault	angreifen/überfallen, Überfall/Angriff
atrocity, atrocious	Gräueltat, entsetzlich/grauenhaft
carnage	Blutbad/Gemetzel
civil unrest	Bürgerunruhe/n
to combat, combat	bekämpfen, Bekämpfung
contagious, contagion	ansteckend, Ansteckung/Seuche
to contain a disease	eine Krankheit kontrollieren
to contaminate, contamination	verseuchen/verunreinigen, Verseuchung/Verunreinigung
to contract a disease	sich eine Krankheit holen/sich anstecken
to converge, convergence	sich angleichen/annähern, Konvergenz/Angleichung
to decline, decline	zurückgehen/senken, Rückgang/Talfahrt
deliberate (vs. accidental)	absichtlich/gewollt
to deport, deportation	abschieben, Abschiebung
to deprive of, deprivation	berauben/vorenthalten, Entzug/Aberkennung
developing countries	Entwicklungsländer
to displace, displacement	vertreiben, Vertreibung
exodus	Aus-/Abwanderung
to donate money, donation	Geld spenden, Spende
emerging countries	Schwellenländer
equilibrium, equilibrated	Gleichgewicht/Balance, gleichgewichtig
to eradicate, eradication	beseitigen/ausmerzen, Beseitigung/Ausmerzung
to even up, even	ausgleichen, ausgeglichen/gleich
to extinguish, to go extinct, extinct, extinction	auslöschen, aussterben, ausgestorben, Aussterben/Untergang
to famish, famine, famine-ridden, to die of famine	verhungern, Hungersnot, von Hungersnot heimgesucht, hungers sterben
to flout rules	sich über Regeln hinwegsetzen
to fuel crime	Straftaten schüren/verstärken
to fundraise	Spendengelder einsammeln
to govern, governance	leiten/regulieren, Führen und Überwachen
(to voice a) grievance	einen Missstand/eine Kränkung (äußern)
humanitarian assistance	humanitäre Hilfe
illiterate (vs. literate) person	Analphabet/in
inclusive (vs. exclusive)	offen/für jedermann frei zugänglich
incubation period	Inkubationszeit
law-abiding	gesetzestreu
(to risk) life and limb	Leib und Leben (riskieren)

to live in a limbo state	in einer Art Schwebezustand/Grauzone (in einem Rechtsvakuum) leben
mortality rate	Sterberate
to neglect, neglect, negligible	vernachlässigen, Vernachlässigung/Unterlassung, belanglos/nebensächlich
outbreak, to break out	(Krankheits-) Ausbruch/Epidemie, plötzlich auftreten
(moral) outrage	(moralische) Entrüstung
to overlord, overlord	überwachen/beherrschen, Ober-/Lehensherr
pandemic	weltweite Epidemie
(engineered) pathogen	(labortechnisch entwickelter) Krankheitserreger
to perpetrate, perpetrator	ein Gesetz übertreten, Straftäter/in
to persist, persistent conflict	fortbestehen, Dauerkonflikt
to postulate goals	Ziele postulieren/für unabdingbar erklären
(to take) precautions	Vorsichtsmaßnahmen (ergreifen)
to prevent, prevention, preventive measure	verhindern/vorbeugen, Vermeidung/Verhütung, Präventivmaßnahme
to push people into poverty	Menschen in die Armut treiben
to rape, rape, rapist	vergewaltigen, Vergewaltigung, Vergewaltiger/in
refuge, to seek/take refuge, refugee	Asyl/Zuflucht, Zuflucht suchen/finden, Flüchtling
to rig rules	Regeln zum eigenen Vorteil beeinflussen
safety concerns	Sicherheitsbedenken
sanitation	sanitäre Anlagen
to squander hopes	Hoffnungen verspielen/vertun
to sustain, sustainable, sustainability	unterstützen/aufrechterhalten, nachhaltig, Nachhaltigkeit
to threaten, to pose a threat	bedrohen/gefährden, eine Bedrohung/Gefahr darstellen
to transmit, transmission	übertragen, Übertragung
to torture, torture	foltern, Folter
to underestimate (vs. to overestimate)	unterschätzen/unterbewerten
undocumented immigrants	illegale Einwanderer
worst-case (vs. best-case) scenario	GAU/größter anzunehmender Unfall

Mapping and Modifying Life: Multiple Risks for Our Planet and Us	
to abolish, abolition	abschaffen, Abschaffung
carbon dioxide	Kohlendioxid
to comply with formalities	(formale) Vorschriften befolgen/einhalten
to deceive, deceptive, deception	betrügen/täuschen, betrügerisch, Betrug
deep water drilling	Tiefseebohrung
to deluge, deluge	überfluten, Sintflut
to deny, denial, denier	leugnen, Leugnung, Leugner/in
to desiccate, desiccation	austrocknen, Austrocknung
to destroy, destructive, destruction	zerstören, zerstörerisch, Zerstörung
to disintegrate, disintegration	zerfallen/sich abbauen, Zerfall
to dislocate, dislocation	Umsiedeln, Umsiedlung

to disrupt, disruption	auseinanderbrechen, Zusammenbruch
to dissipate, dissipation	vergeuden/verschwenden, Vergeudung/Verschwendung
to distress financially	in finanzielle Bedrängnis geraten
drought	Dürre
to endanger, endangered species	gefährden, bedrohte Art/en
to establish minimum standards	Mindeststandards festsetzen
to exploit, exploitation, exploitive competition	ausnutzen/-beuten, Ausbeutung, Konkurrenz durch Ausbeutung
to flood, flood, flood-prone	überfluten, Hochwasser/Überschwemmung, hochwassergefährdet
fossil fuels	fossile Brennstoffe
fracking	hydraulische Frakturierung von Gesteinsschichten zur Energiegewinnung
to garner attention/support	Aufmerksamkeit/Unterstützung gewinnen
to generate electricity	Strom erzeugen
genetically engineered/modified/enhanced	gentechnisch manipuliert/modifiziert/verbessert
greenhouse effect	Treibhauseffekt
habitat	Lebensraum/Biotop
to hamper	behindern/hinderlich sein
to hoax, hoax	weismachen/einen Bären aufbinden, Schwindel/falscher Alarm
inconvenient (vs. convenient) truth	unangenehme Wahrheit
inhospitable/uninhabitable environment	menschenfeindliche/unbewohnbare Umwelt
insignificant (vs. significant)	unbedeutend/unwesentlich
irreversible impact	irreversible/unumkehrbare Auswirkungen
livestock	Viehbestand
mandatory labelling	verpflichtende Kennzeichnung (der Waren)
mean sea level rise	durchschnittliche Erhöhung des Meeresspiegels
to melt, glacier/ice melt	schmelzen, Gletscher-/Eisschmelze
to modify (life)	(Leben) modifizieren/verändern
to obliterate, obliteration	auslöschen/vernichten, Auslöschung
obstacle to trade	Handelshemmnis
to peril, peril, perilous	riskieren, Gefahr/Risiko, (lebens-) gefährlich
precious resource	kostbare/wertvolle Ressource
precipitation	Niederschlag
profligate, profligate	verschwenderisch, Verschwender/in
property rights	Eigentumsrechte
to prosper, prosperous, prosperity	florieren, florierend, Wohlstand
to ration water	Wasser rationieren
referendum	Volksentscheid
to refute a claim/theory	eine Forderung/Theorie widerlegen
to replicate, replication	kopieren, Kopie
resource-efficient	ressourcenschonend

rogue protein	defektes/fehlerhaftes Protein
scare tactics	Angstmacherei
selective breeding	Zuchtwahl
to set a record	einen Rekord aufstellen
to tap groundwater	Grundwasser anzapfen/abgreifen
unprecedented in the history of	beispiellos in der Geschichte (einer Sache)
to up the ante	den Einsatz erhöhen/noch einmal nachlegen
wildlife conservation	Tierartenschutz
to yield (better) crops	(bessere) Ernte(-erträge) einbringen/-fahren

Building a Global Mindset: The Globalization of the Individual	
to adapt to, adaptability	sich anpassen an, Anpassungsfähigkeit
to align with	in Einklang bringen mit
appalling conditions	fürchterliche Bedingungen
average life expectancy	durchschnittliche Lebenserwartung
to break the homogenous cycle	den immer gleichen Kreislauf beenden
college placement application	Bewerbung um Studienplatz
to compete with, competitive, competition	sich messen mit, wettbewerbsfähig, Wettbewerb
cosmopolitan/global citizen	Weltbürger/in
cross-cultural understanding	interkulturelles Verständnis
diverse, diversity	verschiedenartig, Vielfalt
to embrace one's identity	die eigene Identität umarmen/akzeptieren
to engage accountability	Verantwortung zeigen
environmental awareness	Umweltbewusstsein
to expand one's mind/horizon	sein Bewusstsein/seinen Horizont erweitern
fair-trade items	fair gehandelte Ware
fluent, fluency	flüssig, Leichtigkeit (im sprachlichen Ausdruck)
to follow suit	dem Beispiel folgen
formative years	Entwicklungsjahre
to gain practical skills/experience	praxisnahe Fertigkeiten/Erfahrung erwerben
global mindset	weltumspannende Denkweise/Mentalität
to go viral	sich wie ein Lauffeuer verbreiten
to instil an idea	eine Idee einflößen
internship	Praktikum
language proficiency	Sprachbeherrschung
lingua franca	Verkehrs-/Verständigungssprache
philanthropic, philanthropist	menschenfreundlich, Menschenfreund/in
to procrastinate, procrastination	Dinge aufschieben, Verschleppungstaktik
to purchase, purchase	erwerben/kaufen, Erwerb/Kauf
to stifle innovation	Neues im Keim ersticken
to strive to be different	sich bemühen, anders zu sein
sweatshop	Ausbeuterbetrieb
temporary contract	Zeitvertrag

ZOOM IN: Task Instructions (*Operatoren*)

Every exam you take in English consists of three tasks referring to three different performance standards (*Anforderungsbereiche, AFB*).

AFB I: Comprehension

Aspects to be considered:

- introduce your text by giving the essential information about the text at hand (author, title, text type, topic, publication, place, year, intention/target audience)
- use objective and neutral language
- use present tense and avoid contracted forms
- paraphrase (use your own words and do not use specific vocabulary which is also used in the text)
- make sure that your text is not longer than the original one
- do not state your own opinion
- do not quote

Task instruction	Definition
describe	Give a detailed account of something.
outline	Give the main features, structure or general principles of a topic, omitting minor details.
state	Specify clearly.
present	(Re-)structure and write down.
point out	Find and explain certain aspects.
summarise, write a summary	Give a concise account of the main points.

AFB II: Analysis

Aspects to be considered:

- use objective and neutral language
- use present tense and avoid contracted forms
- focus only on specific parts of the text
- stick to the appropriate terminology for analysing texts
- look at the structure of the text and the stylistic devices and explain the resulting function/effect (one very effective method for doing this is the TEE-method)

T(hesis)	E(xample)	E(xplanation)
The author makes frequent use of alliteration/enumeration/metaphor/anaphora/...	quote from the text	His/her intention is to emphasise/stress/underline ...
In addition, he/she underlines his/her point by repeatedly applying contrast ...	quote from the text	These contrasts make clear that ...

Task instruction	Definition
analyse, examine	Describe and explain in detail certain aspects and/or features of the text.
characterise	Describe and examine the way in which the character(s) is/are presented.
examine	cf. analyse
explain	Describe and define in detail.
illustrate	Use examples to explain or make clear.
interpret	Make clear the meaning of something.
compare	Point out similarities and differences.

AFB III: Evaluation

In the third task, you are either supposed to evaluate the text by giving your own opinion (Evaluation), or deal with the given information in a more creative way (Re-creation of text).

Aspects to be considered:
- use present tense and avoid contracted forms
- prove your points with reference to the text by quoting
- clearly state your personal opinion and give reasons for it
- explicitly refer to what you have dealt with in class in regard to the topic

Task instruction	Definition
comment	Clearly state your opinion on the topic and support your views with evidence.
discuss	Investigate or examine by argument; give reasons for and against.
justify	Show adequate grounds for decisions or conclusions.
contrast	Emphasise the differences between two or more things.
assess	Find and explain certain aspects.

AFB III: Evaluation: Re-creation of text

The most common assignment for task three is to transfer the information from the given text into another text type. The text type will depend on whether the original text is a fictional or non-fictional text.

Aspects to be considered:

- use language appropriate for the respective text type (e. g. letter to the editor: formal, conversation/dialogue: (in)formal)
- make a connection to the given text
- be aware of the formal requirements

Task instruction	Definition
write ...	
– a newspaper article (report comment);	Appropriate language/register (report vs. comment) Differentiation concerning – facts, opinions – being objective, personalisation/dramatisation – particular case, context
– a speech script (talk, public/ formal speech, [debate] statement)	Appropriate language/register; Introduction: address of welcome/transparency of structure; Main part: structure and link to text/facts and assessment; Conclusion: e.g. summary/appeal
– a letter/e-mail (formal letter, letter to the editor; personal letter)	Appropriate language/register; author/addressee/reason for writing/form of address/complimentary close; structure: connection to topic, argumentation
– an interview	Appropriate language/register; neutral, unbiased, unemotional interviewer; introduction (topic, conversational partner); structured questioning; conversational partners act according to their role
– an interior monologue/ a conversation – an alternative ending (only advanced course)	Appropriate language/register; coherence between original and continued text

Reading Comprehension: How to Tackle Texts Efficiently

Some texts are harder to comprehend than others are, maybe because the information given is more complex or abstract, the language level higher and more demanding, or the topic unattractive or unfamiliar to you. However, there is no reason to panic. You can tackle even more difficult-looking texts efficiently if you follow some simple rules. These rules include **active reading strategies** that will keep you focussed on the text and make it easier for you to remember what you have read afterwards. The **Five-S Method** is one of those active reading strategies that will help you to improve your reading comprehension skills, i. e. your ability to read a text, process (*verarbeiten*) it, and understand its meaning. The present pages introduce you to this method, to the objectives of each step and the procedure by which these objectives can be achieved. This publication focusses on step five, presenting strategies by means of which you can condense and graphically organise the ideas that you have identified and selected as key points of the text.

The Five-S Method (**S**kim – **S**can – **S**elect – **S**lurp [*schlürfen*] – **S**ummarise)[1]

1. The first time you read a text, **skim** it quickly to get an overview of how the material is organised.
   √ Pay attention to the introduction, the first and last sentences of each paragraph, heading and sub-headings, to get the general idea.
   √ Cast a glance at images, maps, graphs, charts, diagrams and their captions, if there are any.
   In the beginning, the text may seem difficult to you but do not let this make you feel insecure. In four further steps, you will re-read and process the material so that what you need to know for the particular purpose will become clearer and clearer.

2. Read the text-related task instructions and make sure you fully understand how to perform the tasks assigned to you. Then **scan** the text for key words and phrases related to your tasks.
   √ Use a pencil to underline or circle what you identify straightaway as important in this regard. You may also highlight those points, but be careful: too much highlighting will hamper (*hinderlich sein*), rather than help.
   √ If you come across something that you do not understand immediately, use a question mark or add a brief question in the margin and come back to it in the next step.

3. Re-read the text in a focussed but still speedy way and **select** the passages that you need to understand in order to follow the task instructions successfully.
   √ Look up unknown words whose meaning you cannot deduce from the context or from other languages you know.

---

[1] Terminology cf. Gwen Gawith, *Power Learning: A Student's Guide to Success*, Mills Publications, Lower Hutt, NZ 1991

√ Hold your pencil ready so you can annotate the text by making notes in the margin or using post-its or a separate piece of paper, e. g.
  – word definitions or synonyms
  – generic terms (*Oberbegriffe*) for examples listed
  – answers to your questions from step 2
  – key words for statements you have identified as significant
  – your thoughts and ideas on these statements.

In the next step, you will continue making notes in more detail.

Succeed

4. Now that you have selected a set of relevant text passages, **slurp** them. You probably know that, in everyday language, the verb 'slurp' means 'ingesting (usually food or drink) with loud sucking noises'. In computer language, 'slurp' is used to designate how to 'process a text file line-by-line'. In a wider sense and applied to the context of reading comprehension skills, 'slurping' is synonymous with 'taking a text in and absorbing it'. In this step of in-depth reading, you process the content thoroughly and critically.
   √ Take your time while reading each of the text passages you have selected in step 3, then cover up the passages one after the other and ask yourself questions on the text.
   √ Transform the key points of each passage into note form. Test yourself by putting the text away and jotting down these points from memory. Go back to the text to fill in gaps, if necessary.
   √ After reading all relevant passages and making notes, pay attention to the basic structure of the text to find out how the different parts fit together. Look for 'signposts' – phrases like 'most importantly', 'in contrast', 'on the other hand' – that will help you to spot the writer's line of argument and intention. Insert arrows or other symbols to indicate references between text elements.
   √ Remember that your notes should be personalised – do not copy word for word – and briefer than the original. Do not worry about whether anyone else can make sense of your 'scribble'; you are the only person who needs to decipher it.

5. By now, you have probably made so many annotations that you cannot see the wood for the trees. **Summarise**, i. e. condense, your notes and organise them graphically so that they represent the gist of what the task instructions want you to focus on. Be careful, though: not all forms of visualisation are equally suited for each task. Here are some suggestions on how to find the one best suited to a specific task.

   → One of the most frequently used task instructions asks you to **compare** something and point out similarities and/or differences (e. g. p. 49, M 7a & b, task 6).
     √ Use a **table** if you opt for a more familiar way to do so graphically.
     √ In case you prefer a more vivid visual form, choose the **Venn diagram**, whose overlapping circles disclose similar and different features of subjects.

Task instruction:
Compare the situation of Quentina and Fatou.
Illustrate similarities and differences.

Situation of Quentina	Similarities	Situation of Fatou
Evaluation:		

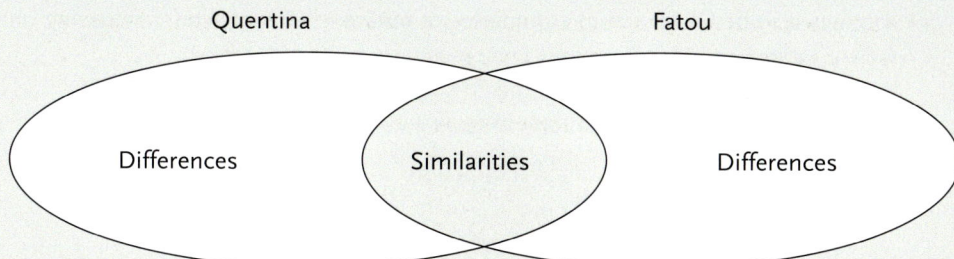

Quentina   Fatou

Differences   Similarities   Differences

Evaluation:

→ Or you are assigned to sort, classify or **categorise** textual information (e. g. p. 28, M 1, task 3).
   √ Arrange the categories and sub-categories in the form of a **tree diagram**, a tree-like graph emphasising the hierarchical nature of a structure.
   √ Alternatively, visualise your classification by means of a **word web** or **mind map**, which are, basically, the same. The core difference between the two is that, in contrast to the mind map, the word web is without pictures and symbols.

Task instruction:
The scientific study **classifies** global risks into four categories:
current risks, exogenic risks, emerging risks, and global policy risks.
Decide which **category** each of the twelve risks belongs to and explain why.

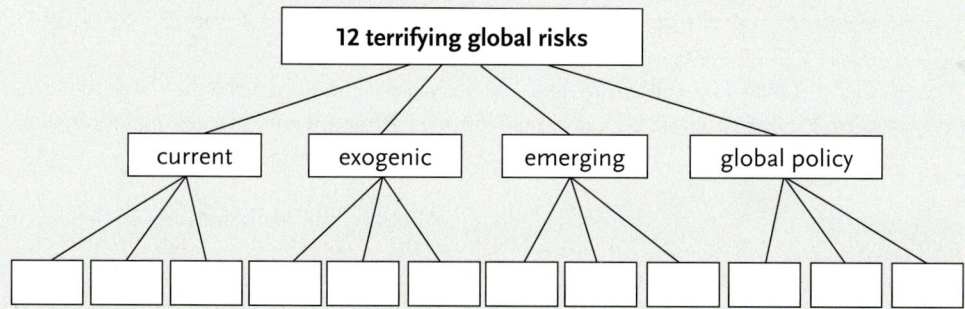

12 terrifying global risks

current   exogenic   emerging   global policy

Explanation:

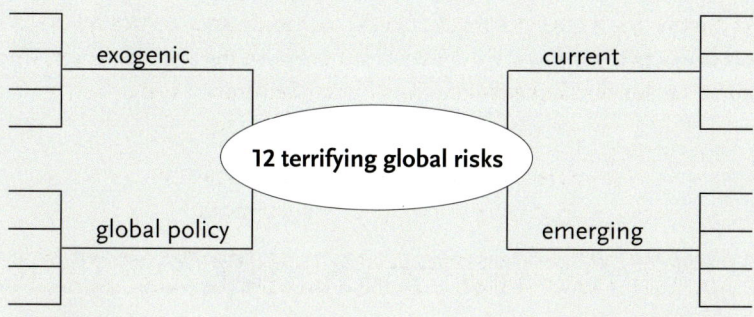

exogenic   current

12 terrifying global risks

global policy   emerging

Explanation:

→ You may also be instructed to summarise or **outline** chains of action, focussing on the chronology of procedures and processes (e. g. p. 19, M 6, task 2).
√ Display simple sequences of events in a **sequence diagram**.
√ Settle for a **flow chart** if you want to outline a more complex course of action.

Task instruction:
Outline a typical evening out at a restaurant with his girlfriend, as presented by the narrator.

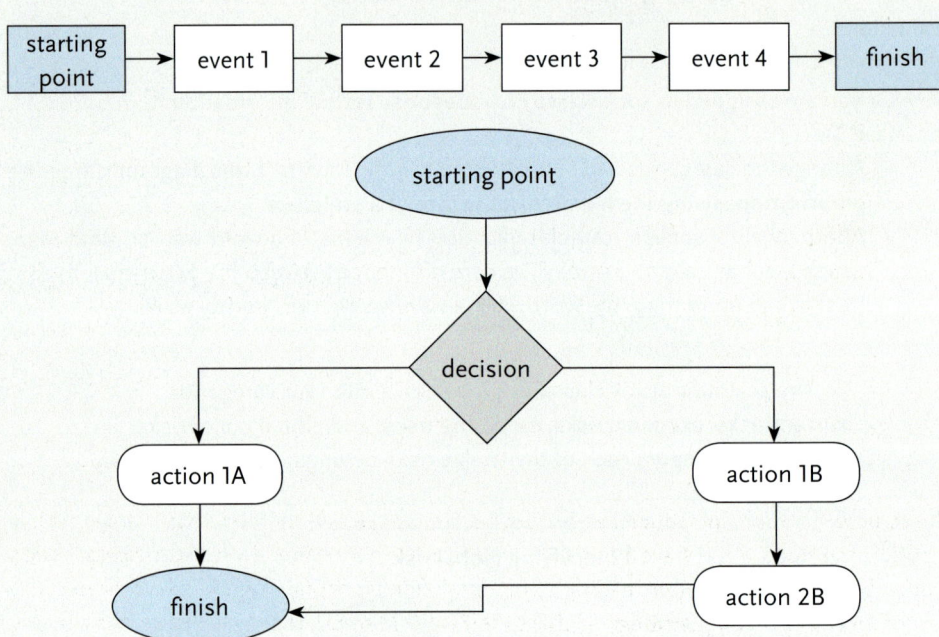

→ Then there are those tasks requiring that you point out or **explain** cause-and-effect or means-and-end relationships (e. g. p. 35, M 3, task 1).
√ Select a **circle chart** if you are to concentrate on the (vicious) cycle of events.
√ Whenever you want to explain more complex relationships, try out the **fishbone diagram**. In contrast to the circle chart, this form of graphic does not primarily tailor to the succession of events but to the juxtaposition of causes/means and effects/purposes.

Task instruction:
What is poverty? Is it simply the lack of money?
And why does being poor mean living in a vicious circle? Try to answer these questions
with a partner and present your results in a structured way.

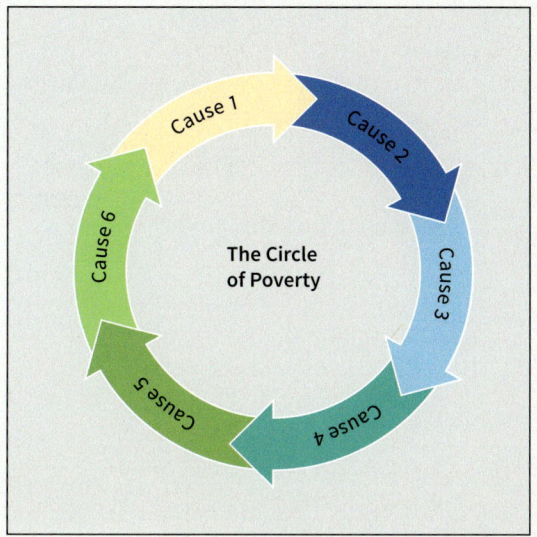

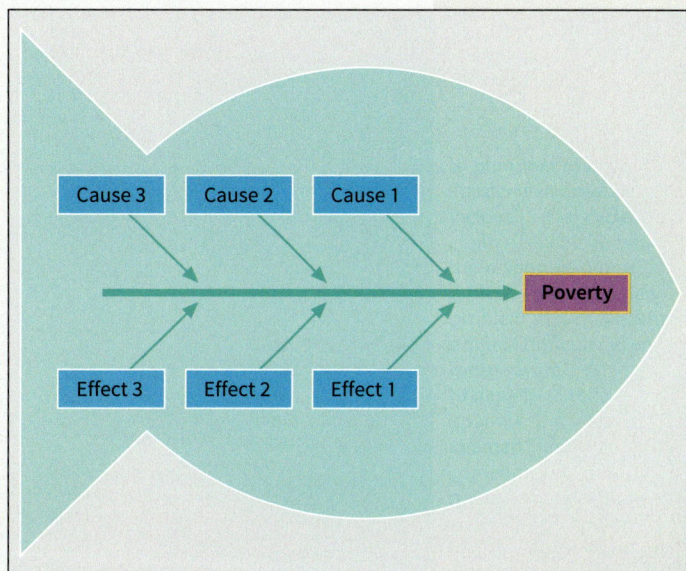

The structuring tools introduced above are but a small selection from a wide range of visu-alisation methods. They have been chosen exclusively with the aim of enhancing perfor-mance and efficiency of your reading comprehension. If applied regularly and properly as part of an **active reading strategy** such as the **Five-S Method**, they will ensure that you un-derstand even the most complicated texts and make the most of the time you spend studying.